Praise for *TrendSmart*

"Once again, Louis Patler tells it like it will be. He tells it with wit and wisdom, his book both a crystal ball and a magnifying glass. The vision he imparts and specific examples he gives illuminate the path to profitability in business. By focusing the present, he has written a history of the future. Your customers are praying that you'll read it"
—Jay Conrad Levinson, author of the *Guerrilla Marketing* series

"Louis Patler has always been alert to shifts in trends and now he shows you how to tell the difference between the flavor of the month and real developments that you can make into personal and business opportunities. He even gives you a glimpse of some of these upcoming trends."
—Florence Stone, editorial director, AMA

"Louis Patler's uncanny ability to make sense out of the non-sensical, define the ill-defined, simplify the complex, and anticipate the future sets him apart from today's visionary 'gurus.' In *TrendSmart*, he offers us incredibly useful tools, tips, and new ways of thinking about what tomorrow may bring in a way that is readily understandable and more importantly immediately applicable. This book is a must-read for anyone who needs to stay ahead of the curve in making critical decisions affecting their business, professional, and personal lives."
—Stephen L. Cohen, Ph.D., vice president and managing director, Learning & Performance Solutions Carlson Marketing Group

"What does the future hold for our plans? No one knows; however, Louis Patler's *TrendSmart* gives us strategies to let us change with the times and accomplish our goals."
—Mille Hughes-Fulford, NASA astronaut

"In order to see TO where we want to go we need to see THROUGH the confusing currents around us. Louis Patler is a contemporary 'seer,' with a gift for both."
—Betsy Raskin Gullickson, consultant and formerly partner of Ketchum, a global public-relations agency

"Once you hold the key to important information, the only thing there is to do is share it. This book gives you the opportunity to see through the eyes of a strategist, poet, and visionary. By sharing his exhaustive research and brilliance, Louis teaches

us how to transform trends into smart business decisions thus enhancing our leadership and making us not just trend savvy but *TrendSmart.*"
—Holly Stiel, author of *Neon Signs of Service*

"*TrendSmart* is a joyride. Packed with fun facts, playful practices, and sassy seriousness, it cranks your mind to the red line. At a time when there is too much junk science passing itself off as future prognostication, *TrendSmart* offers everyday examples of what ordinary high-performers are doing to keep their feet on the ground while they have their heads in the clouds. Louis Patler wittily engages us in an entertaining exploration of the world that is taking shape around us, and then he gives us sailing lessons on how we can navigate through it. You'll not only get great value from reading *TrendSmart,* you'll have good time getting it."
—Jim Kouzes, coauthor of *The Leadership Challenge* and chairman emeritus, Tom Peters Company

"Patler provides the 'down the middle' trend perspectives and insights that 80 percent of industry leaders need and want—neither the macro feel good, 'so what' macro trends nor the belly button lint of the micro trend spotters."
—Matt Levine, CEO & managing director, SourceUSA

"Patler's observations and conclusions on trends and their importance as a business tool, together with his actionable tactics on using those trends, make *TrendSmart* the indispensible leadership guide for today challenging—and exciting—business climate."
—Claire McAuliffe, principal, M^2, Inc.

"I found that *TrendSmart* gave me new tools to spot trends and new insights into business too. There's only one statement in the whole book that rang untrue to me: 'Good information about the future is hard to find.' No it isn't. It's right here in book form."
—Mike Moser, author of *United We Brand*

"As the business of high technology is increasingly interwoven with our lives, Louis Patler's ability to clearly identify the trends that drive fundamental demand for products and services provides the beacon needed to hit technology home runs. Now we know where 'they' will be, before we build it."
—Bill Hoppin, vice president of marketing and strategic sales, Accelerant Networks

"Unlike many consultants, Louis Patler is immersed in the real world—he takes the time to understand, he rolls up his sleeves and becomes a part of the solution. We

worked as partners to transform a company, achieve unprecedented results, and establish a foundation for continued success. This book captures the essence of his unique perspective, his keen ability to spot important trends, and the practicality of 'having been there and done that.'"
—Linda Parker Hudson, president, General Dynamics ATP

"*TrendSmart* is a must-read for anyone serious about moving a business into the 21st century. The choice is simple; follow Louis Patler's roadmap or risk becoming irrelevant."
—Ed de Castro, chairman/CEO (retired), Data General, Inc.

"An insightful 'must-read,' especially for businesspeople and entrepreneurs who are striving to be the first with the next big idea. Through this book we learn how to be a *TrendSmart* consumer, leader, or employee and we are better able to understand and predict how change occurs that will lead us to tomorrow's realities. For those who don't want to miss the next wave."
—Dr. B. Lynn Ware, president and CEO, Integral Training Systems, Inc.

"You'll get from *TrendSmart* what you always get from Louis Patler's books: new ways to think about business, practical application of these insights, and a wealth of references to people and ideas on the leading edge of business innovation. Well researched and well written, Patler's insights will translate into immediate action for the leader, the employee, and the consumer. Read it, enjoy it, use it."
—Patrick McGeary, vice president of human resources, Fidelity Investments

"*TrendSmart* is the first book that really defines the management and marketing issues in today's multigenerational marketplace. The book's format and presentation make for easy reading. Well worth the time."
—George Bull, CEO, Redwood Trust, Inc

"Louis Patler is a master storyteller and strategist. In his latest book, *TrendSmart*, he persuasively argues that understanding customer trends is a necessary component of strategic thinking. He makes the highly complex process of strategic planning much simpler by integrating trend analysis with strategic thinking. Louis uses wonderful anecdotes to illustrate that trend forecasting is not merely jumping on the latest 'fad.' It involves a keen understanding of generational values, historical conditions, and customer behavior across multiple industry sectors. This book is a must-read for futuristic-minded leaders in today's unsettled business climate."
—Anthony Vidergauz, president/CEO, California Closet Company, Inc.

"Louis' message is not a crystal ball, rather a ball of crystals on which he shines his light helping us to capture the opportunities and 'trends' present for sustainable business success. The *TrendSmart* way arms us with future-oriented data and an understanding of the needs and values of our people and customers that allows a business to create opportunity and become the breeding ground for its success."
—Ann Buzzotta, People Skills International

"Louis Patler has this uncanny ability not just to see and assess broad behaviors among a maze of data points, but, most importantly to synthesize these into simple, easily understood, compelling trends. In turn, these trends serve as critical focal points for a broad range of business purposes (e.g., grouping prospects, communication approaches for distinct client groups, etc.)."
—Chris Shipp, vice president, Charles Schwab

"Once again Louis Patler is holding the time warp open for you. 'Break-IT' thinking got your attention; 'Tilt the Field' pointed you in the right direction, and now *TrendSmart* yanks you by the lapel. If you don't pay attention to what Louis has to say here, you're looking down the wrong end of the entrepreneurial telescope."
—Bernie Nagle, coauthor, *Leveraging People and Profit: The Hard Work of Soft Management People and Profit: The Hard Work of Soft Management*

"My chosen field, that of personal financial advisement with a major, national firm, is increasingly and intensely competitive. Anything that helps me anticipate more accurately and respond more quickly is of enormous value. In his new book, *TrendSmart*, Louis Patler provides a rich context for identifying future trends and glimpsing what's ahead. Louis hands us all a piece of good lucky this year if we'll just take it!"
—Stephanie Twomey, Merrill Lynch

TREND SMART

The 21 Trends That Will Change the Way You Do Business

LOUIS PATLER

SOURCEBOOKS, INC.®
NAPERVILLE, ILLINOIS

Published by Sourcebooks, Inc.
P.O. Box 4410, Naperville, Illinois 60567-4410
(630) 961-3900
FAX: (630) 961-2168
www.sourcebooks.com

ISBN 1-4022-0316-0

Library of Congress Cataloging-in-Publication Data

Patler, Louis.
TrendSmart: the 21 Trends That Will Change the Way You Do Business / by Louis Patler.
p. cm.
Includes bibliographical references and index.
ISBN 1-4022-0168-0 (alk. paper)
1. Consumers' preferences. 2. Marketing. 3. Consumption (Economics). I. Title: Trend
smart. II. Title.
HF5415.32 .P38 2003
658.8'343—dc21

2003009658

Printed and bound in the United States of America
BG   10   9   8   7   6   5   4   3   2   1

To the poets of the world
Who have always
Seen things first

Acknowledgments

Where do I begin? I am indebted to so many for so much that if there were a debtor's prison for authors, I would be serving a life sentence.

This said, I forge on undaunted to give credit where credit is due. John Willig, my agent, believed in me and in this book without hesitation. His wisdom and generosity with both time and insight gave me an emotional boost more than once.

To my colleagues at *Near Bridge, Inc.*, especially Ken Beller and Steve Weiss, many thanks for their support in the latter stages of this project. Mike Moser, man for all seasons, fellow author (Cambridge, MA: *United We Brand*. Harvard Business School Press, 2003.) and friend, offered his considerable wisdom at every stage of the book, particularly on the "Instant Branding" chapter. Of course, the final responsibility for the content of this book falls to me.

Peter Lynch at Sourcebooks made the editing and publishing process a complete joy. The entire Sourcebooks team understood the concept and audience for this book from day one.

Laurie Masters made so many contributions to *TrendSmart* that it literally would have been impossible to have completed it by the deadline without her editing skills. She tracked seven iterations, hundreds of articles and footnotes, information on more than two hundred companies, and put in dozens of fourteen-hour days…all with tremendous professionalism, and many hilarious stories that kept us going. To Tom Power, kudos for his experienced eye and understanding of the potential of this book. To Ruth Mills, many thanks for help in early editing of the manuscript from top to bottom.

I must also thank my clients of the past several years. Some business authors, and more than a few academics, do little down-and-dirty, in-the-trenches work with companies. To me, untested ideas are not suitable for a book such as this. Every emerging trend described on these pages comes out of the testing ground of real implementation, in real companies, by real people. Trust me, I do *not* make these trends up! And the tips contained within these covers have seen trial by fire.

I am blessed both to be able to write from experience and to be able to focus on what works. As a professional dilettante—working in many industries with companies as different as American Express, Sun Microsystems, Dell, Del Monte, Fidelity Investments, General Dynamics, Avis Europe, California Closets, Lloyds Bank, the National Basketball Association, and Hewlett-Packard—I have been able to take lessons learned in one place and migrate them to other industries…shamelessly.

I have also learned much from my consulting, training, and keynote speaking, made more than a few mistakes along the way, and come to understand very well that in business it is sometimes better to be useful than "correct." Being unconventional in my methodologies, and being one who likes to "tilt the field" in my favor by bending the rules, I have been fortunate in that my clients have both believed in me and taught me a great deal. The best test, of course, is that many have asked me back!

My debt to poetry, poetics, and poems is incessant. As a small homage, most chapters begin with the words of poets, who hear the Muse of Past and Future sooner than most.

Lastly, to my wife, Catherine, and my children—Kale, Elina, Caitlin, Johana, and Kellin—who tolerated my many travels and long hours away while researching and writing this book: you are true angels in my life.

Table of Contents

The CEO and the Winter Weather

It was late summer, and after a meeting, the staff of a successful venture-capital firm asked their new CEO if the winter was going to be cold or mild. Having a lot of money invested in energy and oil companies, the staff was understandably concerned. "I'll get back to you on that," he said.

Since he was new to the position, he had never been taught "the old secrets" of his predecessor. So, he just looked up at the sky, but, of course, he couldn't tell what the winter weather was going to be. Then, after several days, he got an idea. He went to the website of the National Weather Service and emailed to ask, "Is the coming winter going to be a hard one?"

"The early indications are that this winter is going to be quite cold indeed," the meteorologist at the weather service responded.

So the new CEO went back to his people and told them to invest a bit more in energy companies in order to be ahead of the competition.

A week later, he emailed the National Weather Service again. "Is it going to be an exceptionally hard winter?"

"Yes," the meteorologist again replied. "It's going to be a very cold winter."

The new CEO again went back to his people and told them that at every opportunity they were to put more capital into energy resources.

Two weeks later, he emailed the National Weather Service again. "Are you absolutely sure that the winter is going to be very cold?"

"Absolutely," the meteorologist replied. "It's going to be one of the coldest winters ever."

"How can you be so sure?" the new CEO asked.

The meteorologist replied, "Because the venture-capital firms are pouring money into energy companies like crazy."

The moral of this story? Good information about the future is hard to find!

PART ONE

The TrendSmart Leader

Overview

Trends Are Not Trendy

This book is divided into three parts. Each of these parts organizes trend research and data around a coherent theme. In part 1, the focus is on companies and what TrendSmart™ leaders need to know about cutting-edge trends in organizational development. Part 2 takes a close look at emerging customer trends. In part 3, the light shines on the workforce, illuminating trends that enable the reader to better understand employees.

Each chapter has an oxymoronic—and accurate—title that encapsulates an emerging trend. So, let us get right to it and have a look at why a "real trend" is not at all faddish or trendy. Quite the contrary, a real trend is one that *lasts*, one that moves eventually from emerging trend to profitable, commonsense business practice. The return on investment in this book accrues from gaining both the power of knowing what's coming...*and* what, of what's coming, is here to stay!

Chapter I

Lasting Trends

Where the Future Bypasses the Present

⊕ ⊕ ⊕

"I wanted to know how much information you could give with how
few words just like the lines in a Matisse drawing."
—Diane di Prima

"The biggest lesson in [business] is that it is
going to be a roller coaster."
—Marc Andreessen, chairman of Loudcloud/cofounder of Netscape

The "normal" ebb and flow of a zip-zap, turbocharged world of
business has changed dramatically. Added to this, the quest for
security and predictability have to compete with a growing sense of
uncertainty. The truth is, neither exponential change nor increasing
uncertainty are likely to diminish in the foreseeable future. Today's

workplace is decidedly different, and the new "normalcy" is that exponential change and large mixtures of uncertainty are here to stay.

We now live in a world taken over by ironies, working contradictions, and oxymorons—a world where the line between conventional and unconventional wisdom is drawn with a disposable pen filled with invisible ink. The rules that once seemed so useful, even profound, now wax and wane like a hyperactive harvest moon.

Open the business section of any newspaper or magazine and you see it before your eyes:

- New companies quickly move full circle from not-com to dot-com to hot-com to not-com.
- A five-year-old software company sells for more money than Ford paid to acquire Volvo.
- Top leadership at American Express announces the creation of a new senior-level position: "Vice President of Customer Listening."

How do we become and remain successful in the face of such a dynamic marketplace? How do we know what it takes to thrive in such a chaotic environment? Where do we turn for good information early on?

New times call for new thinking, and new thinking requires new perspectives. This book has been written to offer the reader insights, strategies, and useful tactics to be successful in an uncertain and changing marketplace.

Is That a Real Trend...Or Did You Just Make It Up?

This said, exponential change and economic uncertainty are now old news. The new news is that there are, in the pages that follow, twenty-one significant and lasting trends that are affecting and shaping the nature of business today and for years and years to come. The trends cited, fully understood, provide a strong foundation for competing in a volatile world.

Still, in the face of such challenges, the need for good information—or more specifically, the value of *predictive* information—has never been greater. At my company, Near Bridge, Inc., our focus is on finding useful information that makes the journey from point A to point B easier than you might think. We pride ourselves on knowing a trend from a fad, as well as how to put trend information to strategic, and profitable, use.

With more than twenty years in the trend-spotting business, using proprietary methodologies and curious minds to help with the research, I have learned many lessons that are shared in this book. In the pages that follow, you will hear about more than two hundred companies and two hundred individuals who were tracked, interviewed, and/or monitored as part of a four-year research project for this book.

Using both secondary (Web searches, data analysis, reviews of the literature in the field, etc.) and primary research (focus groups of nearly nine hundred respondents, eighty-two in-depth interviews with executives, and a proprietary database), I developed a list of nearly forty key trends and selected the twenty-one that were most suited for this book. Most of the other trends not found in these pages were more global and would best be the basis of another book at another time. Among these trends were mass urbanization (soon more than 50 percent of the world's population will live in fifty mega-urban areas of the world); rising global micro-political activism; the Euro Decade (rising prominence of the European Union); rising nesting; WordLab (the rise of global experimentation from cloning to clowning); and Mind connect (Web space connectivity based on Minds, not just documents). For an excellent insight into some of these more global trends, see architect Rem Koolhaus's editing of *Wired* magazine, June 2003.

One of my favorite poets, Robert Creeley, wrote an essay that shaped my outlook on trend research. The title of the essay was the inspiration for this chapter. In looking at poems he had written, someone once asked him: "Was that a real poem, or did you just make it up?" His answer made clear what a "real" poem is.

One could say the same thing about trends: *Is that a real trend...or did you just make it up?* My objective is to make clear what trends really are, which trends are going to last over the long haul, and to explain to you *how to use them individually and in combination to become successful.* Those who do so are those I call *TrendSmart.*

TrendSmart Leaders

I trust that by the time you finish reading, you will have a better understanding of the nature of trends—particularly how contrarian and counterintuitive trends can be and how subtly they interact with one another.

Certainly, the ability to understand trends is a useful tool in any leader's toolbox. But the ability to know how to use emerging trend data makes you a *TrendSmart* leader. Many trends have emerged in recent years that will, when properly understood, become the foundation for future success. The trends identified in this book do not exist in isolation. Rather, the real power of trend spotting accrues to those who see the emerging opportunities that come when trends intersect.

Truth be known, the twenty-one trends in this book are like small dots that are forming into pictures and changing *how* we work, *where* we work, and even the way we *feel* about the nature of work itself.

These pictures, when viewed from strategic distances, create a wholly new perspective on commerce and the workplace.

TrendSmart leaders of successful companies not only understand trends per se, but in my experience they share other attributes as well. As professionals, at the core of their personalities are several common values and traits. *TrendSmart* leaders are:

- *Self-initiating.* Their entrepreneurial tendencies are such that they adhere to the old adage that it is easier to ask forgiveness than permission. They are action-oriented initiators whose energy and resilience—like water—makes them basic to the life and sustenance of any organization.
- *Project oriented.* Gone are the days of careers, of linear paths up some archaic balsa-wood ladder. Gone are single-minded, one-skilled workers performing repetitive functions over years and years. We are fully committed now to a production methodology where workers are expected—even encouraged and rewarded—for the depth and breadth of what they know and do. And though projects may come and go, skills remain viable, interchangeable, even portable. Therefore, harnessing seemingly disparate "multitasking" skill-sets has become a new asset-management challenge…and opportunity. Managers understand that reining in the new skill-set is not easy, but like a kid saving up for that bike, it is well worth the time and energy.
- *Results and process focused.* As portable skills become assets, and project-based productivity the modus operandi, the logical outcome is a focused work environment.
- *Team players.* They know that they do not have to go it alone, that they are in the company of others—personally

and/or "virtually"—whose complementary skills are needed and valued. *TrendSmart* leaders know that they need others to be productive and to achieve sustainable levels of success sufficient to stave off the pressures of complacency.

TrendSmart Tip: *TrendSmart* leaders are self-initiating, project oriented, results and process focused team players.

Knowing the Trends

In the world of business, the doctrine of growth has to face head-on the realities of uncertainty. This is a book for managers and leaders, young and old. It focuses on emerging trends that are shaping the nature of work and the products and services we offer. In the chapters that follow, I spell out these trends in detail and touch upon how the lessons of these ironic trends are already being implemented in nearly two hundred companies.

In this sense, this book is neither theoretical nor academic. The information contained within these pages is drawn from my two decades of direct consulting and trend-analysis experience "in the trenches" of commerce.

I am also convinced that the real power of this book accrues from the leveraging and combining of the emerging trends. Business today is not conducted in tidy, disparate pieces. Leaders today understand that interdependence, relationships, and ad hoc configurations of people and processes will win the day—and add to the bottom line. Therefore, the emerging, ironic trends you will read about are best understood as fully modular, and they gain added value when they are viewed in light of all the other trends.

Seeking good information, listening, creating good strategy, building a relationship with customers, and finding and keeping good employees all are part of the picture—and will comprise large portions of this book—but, ultimately, the measure of a successful process in today's work environment boils down to four little words: *show me the results.*

In my twenty years of consulting and trend analysis, it has become quite clear to me that good results come from good information gathered early on in the development of a "big idea" that guides the creation of products and services, as well as the creation of a "brand roadmap." This process is discussed in much more detail as the book unfolds.

TrendSmart Tip: Gather good trend information in order to create good strategy.

In times of prosperity and plenty, good information is important. In times of uncertainty, good information will, literally, make or break your future. I believe that this book offers good information— "good" because it is accurate, practical, and implementable. In uncertain times, there is no need to reinvent the wheel.

TrendSmart Leaders, Consumers, Employees, and Tips

This book is organized into three parts that offer fresh insight into the *TrendSmart* leader, the *TrendSmart* consumer, and the *TrendSmart* employee. Even so, each chapter is written so that it is self-contained and modular such that the interaction and combination of trends may be discovered. *TrendSmart* leaders will appreciate the irony of each trend, subsumed in the title of each chapter. They will also understand the power of such contrarian and predictive information. Several of the chapter trends have been around for some time and are here to stay; others are new and emerging, appearing for the first time within these pages.

To provide an easy summary of some of the key lessons learned from each trend, TrendSmart Tips are found at the end of each chapter.

These tips offer a quick "how to" checklist and are set apart from the regular text.

In the Trenches, Out of the Box

This is a book written to fill a void I found repeatedly in my consulting work with top leaders of complex companies. From my firsthand experience, I saw how difficult it was for them to find strategically useful information. In the world of trend analysis, there is a large area between the sweeping macro trend spotting of a John Naisbitt or a Faith Popcorn and the micro trends from industry experts like Yankee Consulting or Gartner Group. The former (macro) can be too vague, and the latter (micro) too specific. It has been my observation and belief that it is in the middle where most leaders make crucial decisions. This book is written with the practical needs of such business leaders in mind. And today, leadership is not restricted to the CEO or COO…it has become everybody's everyday job. This book combines sound analysis with out-of-the-box creativity:

- It is results oriented.
- It focuses on real people in real companies.
- It looks for a balance of the practical and the strategic, because *innovating for results* is the name of the game.
- It seeks to add value on every level of the business process.

TrendSmart Tip: A trend is not a trend unless it both spans industries and has the potential to affect wide-ranging population groups for a long period of time.

The tone of the book is intentionally conversational, and I have kept business jargon to a minimum. The sources used in the pages that follow are as eclectic as trend spotting and are often *way* "outside the box." You will read fictional parables, excerpts from emails, verbatim case studies, chat room–like discourses, systematic interviews, reviews of articles and books, and firsthand accounts of what today's best and brightest are doing. On a given page, you may find information from the *Harvard Business Review* to *Surfer* magazine to a supermarket tabloid to *American Demographics.*

I believe it is far better to be practical and useful than to be "theoretically correct." Ideas are a dime a dozen, but ideas that people want to buy, and buy into, are very rare. The *TrendSmart* leader, as you will see, learns how to look in unfamiliar places, in unconventional ways, in order to find implementable and profitable ideas and actions.

In my research and experience, emerging trends do not follow a linear or logical path, they affect a wide variety of industries, and they are best "spotted" by those with fresh eyes. One of the most important competitive advantages for any company is having good information about emerging trends. Yet this is an area of considerable confusion, largely because the nature of trends is not well understood. Hence, predicted major "trends" turn out to be short-range fads, aberrations, and/or glitches. Further, most of what passes as "trend spotting" is unnecessarily narrow, focusing industry by industry, region by region, quarter by quarter. In fact, much trend analysis reminds me of the humorous definition of insanity: doing the same thing over and over and expecting different results.

At the very core of good trend analysis is the lesson one learns early on: the past, filtered through the eyes of the present, is of little use in identifying the durable trends of the future. In my twenty years in this field, I've observed that trend spotting requires fresh eyes and focused discipline as well as solid statistical analysis and more than a pinch of intuitive "good lucky" (see chapter 8).

TrendSmart Tip: Most of what passes as "trend spotting" is unnecessarily narrow, focusing industry by industry, region by region, quarter by quarter. Many predicted major "trends" turn out to be short-range fads, aberrations, and/or glitches.

Every *TrendSmart* leader has to be adept at gathering good information in order to create good and useful strategy. Unfortunately, much of what passes as "trend analysis" may seem cutting edge, but has the half life of a weather front—here today, gone tomorrow. Every *TrendSmart* leader understands the difference between that which is "trendy" and that which is a lasting trend. Accurately identifying a real trend from something trendy is, therefore, one crucial ingredient in building a repeatedly successful enterprise.

Further, this book offers valuable insights for foreign leaders and companies interested in a better understanding of the forces affecting the U.S. market. In a global economy, with intense competition for minds, markets, wallets, and purses, international companies who are *TrendSmart* will gain a definite edge on their competitors. In uncertain times, the value and importance of good, predictive information is especially vital. The remainder of this book will describe to you twenty additional working contradictions and lasting trends that are shaping the world of commerce today. These trends do not occur in isolation, and it is the job of the *TrendSmart* leaders to see the interaction and exponential power of combinations of emerging trends.

I am confident that this book will give readers a firm foundation and keen insight into what it takes to build a successful organization in challenging times.

TrendSmart **Tips**

- *TrendSmart* leaders are self-initiating, project oriented, results and process focused team players.
- Gather good trend information in order to create good strategy.
- A trend is not a trend unless it both spans industries and has the potential to affect wide-ranging population groups for a long period of time.
- Most of what passes as "trend spotting" is unnecessarily narrow, focusing industry by industry, region by region, quarter by quarter. Many predicted major "trends" turn out to be short-range fads, aberrations, and/or glitches.

Chapter 2

Visionary Myopia
Where Vision and Results Meet

⊕ ⊕ ⊕

"It seemed, so great my happiness,
That I was blessed and could bless."
—*William Butler Yeats,* "Vacillation"

In today's global marketplace, growth and profitability are deemed critical indicators of success. Public companies are especially under pressure to perform day in and day out, quarter to quarter. It is no wonder that most companies and managers have a span of vision that lasts approximately ninety days. The prevalence of tunnel vision never ceases to amaze me, especially when a broad purview is more suited to the times.

TrendSmart business leaders face double doses of pressure, because they are expected to deliver short-term financial results and create a lasting, successful organization. The emerging and oxymoronic trend I see today for the *TrendSmart* leader is the juxtaposition of a simple, articulate vision and the focused, myopic implementation of that vision. Visionary myopia is that place where the broad vision can truly affect the results, because it moves from the intangible vision to the tangible product or service and then to the bottom line.

The ability to create a vision that is powerful enough to guide strategy and profitability is, in my experience, exceedingly rare. Rather, I frequently see a wordy cliché that lacks both meaning and the ability to engender impassioned commitment. The absence of a strong vision, combined with the pressure for short-term results, makes it very difficult for business leaders to step outside the normal boundaries of conventional wisdom and experiment with a broad, compelling vision. It is no wonder that there is a tremendous fear of making mistakes.

TrendSmart Tip: Use the vision to shape both strategy and implementation.

Ironically, mistakes and miscalculations have long been breeding grounds for new visions and strategies. If you are lucky, you learn from your mistakes and you understand the better and greater use of a miscalculation. Most of us, however, are not so fortunate. Though there are those who are adept at "learning how to back into a clearing," as my mother used to say, more typically, most of us have a tough time seeing the larger picture because we look only at what is close to us. But adding insult to injury, without the bigger picture and vision to guide us, our performance and productivity may suffer.

Not Seeing the Forest for the...Mushroom?

Let me offer an entertaining biological metaphor regarding myopia. Were you to walk through the Malheur National Forest in eastern Oregon, you would be hard pressed to notice "it." Standing under a massive tree, you would not necessarily notice "it" either. But flying over the forest, it would be hard to miss: a mushroom-like fungus, spreading through the roots of trees, that now covers 2,200 acres, making it the largest living organism ever found.[1]

Popularly known as the honey mushroom, the *Armillaria ostoyae* started from a single spore too small to see without a microscope and has been weaving its black shoestring filaments through the forest for an estimated 2,400 years, killing trees as it grows. The outline of the giant fungus stretches 3.5 miles across and extends an average of three feet into the ground. It covers an area as big as 1,665 football fields. No one has estimated its weight.

As big as it is, and standing right on it, it is easy to miss. "When you're on the ground, you don't notice the pattern, you just see dead trees in clusters," said Tina Dreisbach, a botanist and mycologist with the U.S. Forest Service's Pacific Northwest Research Station in Corvallis, Oregon. "There hasn't been anything measured with any scientific technique that has shown any plant or animal to be larger than this," said Gregory Filip, associate professor of integrated forest protection at Oregon State University.

Fields of Dreams

Several years ago, the American film *Field of Dreams* became a box-office success, in part because it captured the imagination of moviegoers. In the film, a young man hears a voice that tells him to construct a baseball diamond in the middle of an Iowa cornfield. Needless to say, his friends and loved ones question his sanity. Undaunted, he follows the voice in his head, which tells him, "If you build it, they will come." "They," in this case, includes a team of deceased baseball heroes, the young man's deceased father, and, by the end of the movie, avid fans as well. Indeed, he built it, and they came—and they paid.

TrendSmart Tip: If you have vision, profits will follow. Don't be afraid to step outside the box and develop a wild, bold idea.

Most of the major success stories of the last century can be reduced to similar logic. If you have the vision, profits will follow. Let's look now at a few examples of individuals who had a dream of their own:

- Priceline.com founder and vice chairman Jay Walker asserts that the Internet revolution hasn't actually begun. When it does, he says, "the race won't look anything like it does today, any more than the pre telephone world looked like the post telephone world.... People who believe that history will repeat itself over and over are typically people who have no vision." Walker's vision for Priceline nearly defies competition. "Every other model [in the Internet space] has a fixed price, like Amazon, or there's a competition among buyers to set price, like eBay. We do neither. We have no bricks and mortar, no warehouses. We're a pricing system."[2]

- Marion McGovern, cofounder of M², used statistical sampling to help her test the validity of her initial idea for M²: the matching of highly experienced interim workers with ad hoc project needs of companies. (See chapter 5 for more on M².) "I sent out surveys to about 1,000 companies and then I had focus groups. I got a resounding 'maybe' from both sides."[3] Though the results of her efforts were inconclusive at best, the voice in her head told her there was value to her vision. "It was difficult to know whether we really had a business. I was once told, 'It's just as bad to be five years too early as five years too late.'" With her vision came not only the creation of a company but also the launch of the interim-staffing industry.

- I served on the board of directors of Fellows Placement, a staffing and temp-to-hire company with offices throughout the United States. Founder and CEO Raejean Fellows found there was utility in gathering consistent and current information on the continually changing needs of clients. Rather than using what she calls a "spray and pray" approach to data gathering, Fellows developed a targeted, succinct internal customer-tracking system. But that was only half the vision. She concurrently created a proprietary software program, called "FingerPrints," which monitored the skills and proficiencies of the temps. With both sets of data in place—on clients and temporary workers—finding a match was much easier, thereby creating a win/win/win for clients, temps, and the agency.

- Great Harvest Bread Co. of Great Falls, Montana, broadened its vision shortly after it opened its doors. "We're a bread company, but we're also a university. We're creating a community of learning," says COO Tom McMakin. "A network of equal participants doing similar things will generate lots of new ideas—and produce a big competitive advantage for the whole company."[4] Although there is an operating manual that details best practices, owners run their bakeries as they see fit—on just one condition: like university professors, owners are expected to share what they learn along the way with other owners in the Great Harvest system.

- PeopleSoft's simple seven-word vision includes the three primary stakeholders in any company: customers, employees, and shareholders. "When we founded PeopleSoft, we had three core principles: Make customers happy. Have fun. Be profitable," says David Duffield, president, chairman, and CEO of PeopleSoft, Inc.[5]

TrendSmart Tip: Keep your vision simple.

- For a vision to guide and produce results, it must be broad, inclusive, and inspiring. It never hurts to have a vision that can capture the imagination of every customer and employee, as well. Consider Nokia: its vision is clear, simple, and articulate. Nokia CEO Jorma Ollila states it for all to hear: "To put the Internet into every pocket."[6]

TrendSmart Tip: For a vision to guide and produce results, it must be broad, inclusive, and inspiring.

Flunking the Visionary

One of the common attributes of visionary leaders is their incredible tenacity and perseverance, even in the face of naysayers and skeptics. Trained as a scientist, legendary visionary Bob Metcalfe had faith in his business vision, even under fire. Scott Kirsner tells an interesting story of Metcalfe's early career that contributed to the eventual founding of Santa Clara, California-based 3Com.

TrendSmart Tip: One of the common attributes of visionary leaders is their incredible tenacity and perseverance.

"Enamored of the [early development and potentials of] Arpanet, Metcalfe made it the topic of his doctoral dissertation. But something surprising happened. Harvard flunked him." His doctoral committee felt it was not "theoretical enough." Graduation invitations had already been sent out, and Metcalfe's parents were set to make the trip to Cambridge from New York. Metcalfe had already accepted a position at Xerox's Palo Alto Research Center.

Reflecting on this years later, Metcalfe says, "I'm even willing to stipulate that it wasn't very good. But I'd still justify my anger at those bastards for letting me fail. Had they been doing better jobs as professors, they never would have allowed that to happen. But I hated Harvard and Harvard hated me."

Metcalfe told his parents. Then he phoned Bob Taylor, head of the computer science lab at PARC and his new boss. "I just failed my defense," Metcalfe told him. He was stunned by Taylor's response. "Come on anyway," Taylor said. "Finish it up out here." What he "finished up" became the start of the Ethernet.

Metcalfe's vision was larger than that of his professors at Harvard, and he stayed with it until he brought it to fruition. And, perhaps to show his disdain for Harvard's tunnel vision, he also made sure Ethernet became an open standard. Harvard remains Metcalfe's object of disdain; Taylor, his hero. "There's nothing Bob Taylor can do wrong," he says.[7]

TrendSmart Tip: Pay less attention to focus groups or other outsiders for validation of your vision; instead, follow your gut instinct.

Visionary Laws

Within the technology community, Metcalfe has the rare distinction of having a "Law" named after him, as does Gordon Moore.

By way of summary, Moore's Law had to do with the increasing complexity of integrated circuits. "I had one goal in mind, and that was to try to get across the idea that integrated circuits were going to be a cheap way to do electronics," says Moore. Metcalfe's Law says that "the value of a network grows as the square of the number of its users."[8]

What I find interesting in both laws is that Metcalfe and Moore had the end user in mind. For Moore, it was making electronic devices available to the masses via integrated circuits. Moore understood mass customization early on. For Metcalfe, it was knowing that the inherent value, and power, of any network is related to the scale of its use.

High-Tech "Comedy"

Of course, for every triumphant story of legendary visionaries and pre-scient laws there are stories that illustrate rampant "underwhelming" myopia. Scott Adams's *Dilbert* comic strip has certainly tapped into a nearly infinite wellspring of examples. Recently, a friend faxed me the winning entries from a business magazine's Dilbert "copycat" contest. Please note: the quotes in Exhibit 2-1 are real; they are not made up.

Exhibit 2-1. Dilbert Meets Corporate Myopia

- "As of tomorrow, employees will only be able to access the building using individual security cards. Pictures will be taken next Wednesday, and employees will receive their cards in two weeks."
- "What I need is a list of specific unknown problems we will encounter. How long is this Beta guy going to keep testing our stuff?"
- "Email is not to be used to pass on information or data. It should be used only for company business."
- "Turnover is good for the company, as it proves that we are doing a good job in training people."
- "This project is so important, we can't let things that are more important interfere with it."
- "Doing it right is no excuse for not meeting the schedule."

We can see from these examples that Dilbertisms are alive and well—even thriving—in the corporate world. I read Dilbert regularly to gain an insight that only humor affords—an unfiltered look into the soul of the work world. Every leader has to find ways to do this in order to know the essence of the enterprise, blemishes and all.

TrendSmart Tips

- Use the vision to shape both strategy and implementation.
- If you have vision, profits will follow. Don't be afraid to step "outside the box" and develop a wild, bold idea.
- Keep your vision simple—for example, PeopleSoft's vision is based on only three core principles and seven little words: "Make customers happy. Have fun. Be profitable."
- For a vision to guide and produce results, it must be broad, inclusive, and inspiring.
- One of the common attributes of visionary leaders is their incredible tenacity and perseverance.
- Pay less attention to focus groups or other outsiders for validation of your vision; instead, follow your gut instinct.

Chapter 3

Generalized Priorities

Where the "Big Picture" Guides Little Decisions

⊕ ⊕ ⊕

"…anyway, it must be obvious, it is the matrix
which interests me more than the metrics."
—Ed Dorn

Strategic thinking is a key skill in today's workplace, and strategic thinking in *TrendSmart* companies is now found at all levels of an organization. Ironically, for many years, "strategy" was used almost synonymously with "theory," and was therefore held apart and kept separate—far too separate—from implementation. Strategy was considered vague at best, and useless at worst. Further, strategic thinkers were labeled as "generalists" and deemed incapable of prioritized and sequential decisions. By analogy, strategists are considered to be good with their heads, not their hands. Today it is clear that setting clear priorities requires the use of head and hands, the linking of the macro and the micro.

Good strategy is therefore aligned with sound processes for implementation. It also provides an overview, a sense of direction, a matrix for prioritization, and a basis on which to make—or shy away from—decisions.

The ability to make day-to-day decisions guided by larger vision creates what I call "generalized priorities." By having generalized priorities, you have established a link between the big picture and the small, practical, daily decisions.

Linking Strategy and Profitability

Good strategy is a pathway to productivity and profitability. The perception of the importance of good strategy and its link to profitability has not come easily. For decades, in fact, conventional business wisdom placed mental barriers between good strategy and high performance. To break down these barriers, my first book, *If It Ain't Broke...BREAK It!* offered readers dozens of instances of where *un*conventional wisdom was the shortest path to profitability.

Nonetheless, conventional wisdom remains the convention. For example, "Never change horses in midstream" almost surely guarantees that you won't be able to change quickly with the times. Would you want to be on an aging horse in a rising river of white-water rapids? The inherent problem with these tried-and-true concepts, however, is that they have indeed been tried but are often no longer true.

Against this backdrop, let us now look at three practical topics affecting strategy formation and change in more detail.[9] First, the assumptions, or "strategic givens," that underlie modern strategic thinking; second, how to recognize "good" strategy; and third, when to change strategy.

The "Strategic Givens"

I call the basic assumptions that underlie a company's strategy its "strategic givens." Though they may differ from organization to organization, these broad assumptions always operate, whether or not they are consciously identified. It is helpful to bring to light these cornerstones of your paradigm. Here are five broad assumptions that I have found to be generally applicable across many industries and national boundaries:

1. *Today, the rate of change is exponential, not incremental.* This is a crucial starting point. Things are changing at a fast-forward, willy-nilly pace. This makes it very difficult to use conventional modes of thought, measurement, or planning. Often things don't build up or add up; they just explode to a new level.

2. *Things will never get "back to normal"; this is normal!* The so-called glory days of the bygone past have gone by fast. And they won't be back. So, to those who cling to the recent past, the new strategic thinkers say: "Get over it! Get used to it! *This* is normal…from now on!"

3. *Plan as we may, the future has plans of its own.* Because exponential change is here to stay, we have to look down the road with 20/20 vision, focusing on the next twenty minutes and the next twenty years simultaneously. The bad news is that the number of senior executives and key managers who possess 20/20 vision is minimal. The good news is this is a learnable cognitive skill that a few training programs, including my program, "TrendSmart Innovating for Results," can teach you.

TrendSmart Tip: Good strategy requires 20/20 vision: focusing on the next twenty minutes and the next twenty years simultaneously.

4. *Organizations that learn how to learn, ask the right questions at the right time, and know how to find the answers will thrive in a global economy.* Astute organizational strategists know that customized methods and responsive processes are more powerful than logical routines and off-the-shelf systems. Asking the right questions *at the right time* will determine the most sustainable and viable answers.

5. *The organizations that will excel are those that value flexibility, diversity, integrity, cooperation, and innovation.* It is no longer sufficient to "add value" to products; we have to add *values* into the process and the product. Customers, creditors, consumers, and our consciences now require it.

TrendSmart Tip: Organizations that will excel are those that value flexibility, diversity, integrity, cooperation, and innovation.

Good Strategy

There is strategy, and then there is good strategy. "Good" strategy is not tactics; it is focused directionality, another way to establish "generalized priorities." By good strategy, I mean strategy that is implementable and drives such things as profitability, growth, and customer loyalty.

Good strategy is the result of understanding the assumptions of your business model; sound investigation; open, curious, and broad thinking; as well as asking the right questions at the right time. Finding the difference between strategy and good strategy rests on an alignment of the answers to the seven fundamental questions below. These are not easy questions to answer, nor are their answers cast in stone. I advise *TrendSmart* leaders to ask these questions—all of them—at least twice a year. Even if the answers have not changed significantly, at minimum you will be thinking on the right level with some regularity. Then, once you have the perspective these answers will offer you, you are ready to make hard decisions because you will know *why* you are doing what you are doing, and your actions will be based on sound strategic thinking.

TrendSmart Tip: Organizations that learn how to learn, ask the right questions at the right time, and know how to find the answers will thrive in a global economy.

Seven Questions That Foster "Good" Strategy

1. *What business are you in?* Many companies are in more than one business and/or offer a variety of products and/or services without knowing it. Others have a single focus or a few well-conceived products or services. It is important to understand the business you are in, the competition, and the most innovative practices in your industry. For example, Sam Walton started Wal-Mart to bring popular brands to smaller communities at low prices.

2. *What* other *business are you in?* Many companies do not see their business through a wide enough lens. They fail to capitalize on other business opportunities that can accrue from little more than a change in thinking. Consider these examples:

   - Trucking companies are in the transportation business—a broader perspective than merely "trucking."

- Banks are in the transaction management business—not just "financial services."
- Professional soccer teams are also in the entertainment business—not just "sports."
- Ford and GM are in the financial-services business—not merely "automotive and truck manufacturing."

3. *What are your core competencies?* Knowing the core competency of your company will give you an incredible competitive advantage. Competencies are not mere strengths. Every company has its strengths, but only a very few strengths are true competencies that give you an edge over the competition—market differentiators that separate you from others. But core competencies are often quite subtle. For example, one billion-dollar computer connector manufacturing company accomplished much of its fast growth via an unnoticed core competency: the ability to acquire companies and hold on to their key employees and customers.

4. *What are your core values?* Isolating and identifying core values is crucial. If your core value is short-term profitability, you need to organize your company accordingly. If you value long-term relationships with customers, this will require a different strategy, compensation program, and organizational chart. What is valued should inform strategy through and through. For example, Southwest Airlines has a people-oriented culture. So, for example, they hire for hospitality and humor skills.

5. *What competitor will be your next partner?* Good strategy is open to realignments, even with a current competitor. It may be to your advantage to form a strategic partnership on a specific product, research and development, or other venture with a competitor in order to remain a player in your own field. When you research a competitor-as-potential-partner, you will see their strengths and weaknesses in a new—and strategically important—light. We see precedent for this in the lobbying efforts of many companies for the collective "greater good" of their industries. For example, upon his return as CEO of Apple Computers, Steve Jobs negotiated a $150 million investment from Microsoft.

6. *Are your short-term goals and long-term strategies aligned?* Public companies tend to think quarter to quarter in order to please financial analysts and shareholders. The problem is that the pressures of meeting the analysts' projections for the next three months too often conflict with the opportunities of the next few years. Companies need to align short-term results with long-term profitability, short-term profits with long-term customer satisfaction. For example, BarclayCard committed the time and resources necessary to move from a strategy based on mass marketing to one of mass customization. In doing so, it gained market share and increased its profitability.

7. *Do your answers to questions 1–6 complement (or negate) one another?* Too often a company will provide a viable answer to only one or two of the above questions. The real advantage, however, goes to the company that consistently aligns its answers to all of these questions.

Dismount or Ride On?

By regularly revisiting these seven questions, you will then have additional, crucial information to detect the early warning signs of "good" strategy that has taken a turn for the worse. If, for example, two or more of your answers to the first six questions change significantly, it is often an early indicator that fundamental shifts in strategy are appropriate.

In the face of constant quarter-to-quarter pressures, it is tempting to abandon a direction prematurely. How many times have you come across companies that have a new process, system, technology, or business plan seemingly monthly? One former client of mine at a major financial-services company refers to this as the "buzzword of the month club."

Companies that frequently change their strategic plans, core products, and organizational charts risk leaving shareholders bewildered, customers underwhelmed, and employees confused. The art of leading a company today relies on the ability to "stay the course" until such time as there is convincing reason to change—evidenced by a new configuration of answers to the seven strategy questions.

Strategy Comes Out of the (California) Closet

Seeing the big picture enables strategic decisions to lead the way to profitability and growth. For example, one of my clients is California Closets, a $200 million company that designs and installs customized closets in homes via a system of more than 150 franchises worldwide. Founded in the late 1980s, it had grown and become profitable over the years, averaging double-digit growth throughout the 1990s via what could best and charitably be described as an informal bureaucracy. CEO Anthony Vedergauz asked me to develop a strategic-planning process for the company, a process—as separate from a strategic plan per se—that would provide headquarters and franchises with a set of core values, core competencies, and core strategies to help shape, direct, and guide growth over the forthcoming decade.

TrendSmart Tip: Creating a strategic planning *process* within the corporate culture is often more important (and more virtual) than having a strategic *plan* per se.

To accomplish this, I began with a lengthy phone survey of nearly a third of the franchisees to determine a baseline of their thinking regarding key issues. I also did the identical survey with corporate staff, then gathered and analyzed the data and shared the results of each survey with both groups. Using content analysis, I was able to help California Closets identify three crucial strategic initiatives, slightly redirect franchisee priorities, create an intranet system for better communication and training, and redefine roles and responsibilities. With these cornerstones in place, the big picture came into view and guided an ongoing series of actionable next steps. Consequently, by articulating the generalized priorities, the outdated bureaucracy was replaced by a flexible organizational structure that more closely resembles what I call an "ad hocracy."

There are times when the rate of change exceeds our ability to grasp it. Never before has change been so dramatic, challenging, and replete with opportunity.

TrendSmart **Tips**

- Good strategy requires 20/20 vision: focusing on the next twenty minutes and the next twenty years simultaneously.
- Organizations that will excel are those that value flexibility, diversity, integrity, cooperation, and innovation.
- Organizations that learn how to learn, ask the right questions at the right time, and know how to find the answers will thrive in a global economy.
- Creating a strategic planning *process* within the corporate culture is often more important (and more virtual) than having a strategic *plan* per se.

Chapter 4

Delayed Urgencies

Where the "Urgent" Is Chronically Delayed and the "Important" Is Consistently Sought

⊕ ⊕ ⊕

"What keeps you young, Jack?"
His reply, "I don't forget to breathe."
—Jack Kirk, 94, at the finish of the 7.5-mile
valley-to-ocean "Dipsea" race.

TrendSmart leaders understand that some things in life are vital, like breathing; other things can wait. It sounds like a simple, obvious understanding—what my children would affectionately refer to as a "DUH!" revelation—but prioritizing is often harder than it might need to be.

TrendSmart Tip: Do what's "urgent" only when what's really important is already done.

Stephen Covey foreshadowed the inability of most managers to keep their priorities straight when he described how often the "urgent" gets in the way of the "important." Applying his concept to time-management issues, Covey convincingly showed how easy it is to put off what really matters—the important—in the face of the incessant, urgent pressures of a given week, day, or morning. To *TrendSmart* leaders, though, the value of Covey's insight extends far beyond time-management issues. How often have you witnessed the urgent beating up on the important in other arenas? For example:

- Strategy is at best relegated to an annual activity for only the most senior executives.
- Wall Street and/or shareholder pressures drive quarterly results to the diminution of long-term, larger gains.
- Meeting sales quotas for acquiring new customers leaves the best customers stranded.

The list goes on.

TrendSmart leaders keep the important at the forefront, look for the bigger picture, and constantly prioritize, such that the urgent gets its due only when the important has been accounted for. This often places such leaders in the role of contrarians, champions of unconventional wisdom. For example, Nestlé CEO Peter Brabeck firmly believes that he is running a company for the long haul, one that will generate a reasonable profit for an incredibly long period of time. To him, a good company evolves "slowly but surely," and consequently his focus is on strengthening those aspects of Nestlé that he feels should essentially stay the same. "That is why," he says, "we see adapting, improving, and restructuring as a continuous process,"[10] a process, ironically, that itself stays the same.

TrendSmart Tip: Keep what's important at the forefront; look for the bigger picture; constantly prioritize and reprioritize.

Brabeck pays little heed to shareholder demands or to Wall Street analysts. Rather, he looks for trends in long-term yield, opportunities for rock-solid, steady profitability. For example, he did not jump on the technology bandwagon. To him, technology is no more than a tool. "Nestlé," he says firmly, "is about people, products, and brands— that's it." He certainly knows what he finds to be important in running a company.

In this sense, Brabeck adheres to the Warren Buffett Way, a long-haul investment/profit strategy based on building upon the power of brand recognition for products with a long history (e.g., gum, razor blades) combined with sound management practices.

TrendSmart leaders are adept at always seeking the important and staving off the incessant urgencies of the day. To these leaders, crisis management or firefighting is anathema…and counterproductive.

It is instructive to look at companies whose *product* is speed to learn lessons about what is important. Take FedEx, for example. A few years back, a revelation occurred: FedEx understood that its customers actually believed their ads and had come to assume that packages would be delivered worldwide, on time. That's the urgent part.

The important part was much more subtle: FedEx developed a customer-friendly tracking system, thereby removing much of customers' emotional anxiety. By allowing customers to find out exactly where in the shipping process *their* package was, FedEx not only alleviated fears, it also made a state-of-the-art distribution system possible.

Avis had an equivalent epiphany. Realizing that the urgent part of its business was having the right car in the right place at the right time, it subsequently had the revelation that its greatest profitability came from its repeat customers. The important was then attended to by initiating a series of special promotions and value-adds for its best customers.

Putting Out Fires...Literally

Most managers—and CEOs for that matter—spend a good chunk of their time "putting out fires" and attending to the urgencies and pressures of operations. But one weekday morning, Pro-Tech Welding's CEO Michael P. Weagley had to take that phrase literally when a blaze broke out at its painting facility. Not one to waste time, within hours Weagley made a few quick calls and had his crew back in business—in the parking lot. Pro-Tech not only made its scheduled shipments for that day but also broke the company's daily production and shipping records.[11]

For some, these "fires" are personal and burn inside. Fast growth means tense times, and tension requires a release. Cynthia B. Kaye, CEO of Logical Choice Technologies, thinks she knows how to take important measures to break the tension caused by the urgent tasks in her daily routines. Some days she rides her cherry-red Harley-Davidson through her company's building. She also likes to "jam" on her electric guitar—over the company intercom. Kaye says her antics tend to "freak out" the new hires at first but that people quickly get used to it. One new manager saw the CEO cycle by in her leathers with her long hair flying and immediately called his wife to say he'd picked the right place to work.[12] By now, though, it is easy to dismiss Harleys and "fun" perks as frivolous dot-com games. Naysayers are having a field day every time a dot-com goes bust. Still, though, there are lessons to be learned from the dot-com experience.

The Bellagio Blitz

Many Silicon Valley companies grew exponentially in short periods of time, and such exponential growth requires that the important consistently prevail over the urgent. In many instances, these companies had to locate and hire employees ten to twenty times more quickly than the industry standard. Wisely, when Las Vegas's Bellagio hotel faced a similar dilemma—needing to hire 9,600 people in twenty-four weeks—it turned to the lessons learned from the dot-com world and, interestingly, the U.S. military.

"The only way that we could hire so many so fast was to move everything online—the entire application process, plus all of the personnel files that resulted from hiring 9,600 people," says Arte Nathan, vice president of human resources. "That meant we had to build one of the first fully integrated online job-application and HR systems....Going online would take out of the loop the people who shouldn't be there: human resources."

The goal was to make the online application system "as easy to use as an ATM," because, he adds, they needed to take in 1,200 applications a day. When you have more than eighty thousand job applicants, probably 20 to 30 percent of them are "just kicking tires; they're only casually interested in the opportunity. But I'm serious about them, because I need to hire 9,600 people. My job is to treat these folks as if they are guests at Bellagio: I want to impress the hell out of them and convert them from casually interested to very interested." So he applied to applicants the same personalized-service principles they used for guests.

Next, they interviewed. And they interviewed. All twenty-seven thousand of them—in ten weeks. Every day, 180 hiring managers conducted a collective average of 740 interviews. "We instructed the managers for a week on how to use the online system and how to complete the interview in thirty minutes." Letting an interview run to forty minutes would have "sent us into a tailspin. So we trained our managers, we made sure that they were ready, and then we hit the bell and took off," says Nathan.

For the interviews, hiring managers asked a set of behavioral questions that had been developed for this process. Candidates were scored based on their answers, which were then ranked in numerical order and fed into the database. They used a formal system. "If we had left it up to 180 managers to follow their own formats, we'd still be interviewing candidates today," says Nathan.

Virtually all of these techniques and the accompanying data-tracking software was tried and tested in the Silicon Valley boom of the 1990s. Perhaps more to the point, their hiring process was reviewed by the U.S. military. "For us, hiring 9,600 people was like Desert Storm," says Nathan. Norman Schwarzkopf actually examined their system, and he said it was "similar to moving a military operation around the globe."[13]

Timely Tips

Day-Timer, the original Palm Pilot, has been in the time-management business for a long time and offers some good advice—see Exhibit 4-1. Granted, we don't all have to hire thousands in a few weeks, but we do have to get through each day.

Exhibit 4-1. 10 Tips for Taking Control of Your Time

1. List everything you need to do today—in order of priority.
2. Make time for *important* things, not just urgent ones.
3. Write your goals. Then write the *steps* to your goals.
4. Set a starting time as well as a deadline for all projects.
5. Slice up big projects into bite-sized pieces.

6. If you run out of steam on one project, switch to another.

7. Say no to new projects when you're already overloaded.

8. Trim low-payoff activities from your schedule.

9. For each paper that crosses your desk: act on it, file it, or toss it.

10. Use a Day-Timer system to manage your busy life.

TrendSmart Tip: Use time-management systems and software to help you achieve your goals and spend your time wisely.

Tapping into Napping

Time management is incessant, too. No longer does it relate only to one's waking hours. *TrendSmart* leaders are often capable of factoring in some sleep to stay fresh for each day. American society is sleep deprived, and the problem is growing. People mistakenly think sleep is a waste of time. They don't realize they'll be more productive if they get more sleep.

Tamar Sherman offers some excellent insights into what some American companies are doing about this:

- Fatigue is to blame for 60 to 90 percent of all industrial accidents and more than one hundred thousand highway crashes a year.
- Sleepy workers cost American companies $18 billion a year in lost productivity, according to a recent survey by the National Sleep Foundation.[14]

Napping on the job is cause for dismissal at most businesses, but there are exceptions:

- An architectural firm in Kansas City, Missouri, Gould Evans Goodman Associates, encourages its employees to take a power nap whenever they feel the need. The company provides purple and turquoise "spent tents" for its architects, designers, and city planners. There is no sign-up sheet and no official policy other than "Do not disturb." Says vice president Karen Gould, "People are very good about it. It's really amazing." There have been no problems.

- Yarde Metals, an aluminum and stainless-steel processing company, has nap rooms with stereo systems, mood music, and soft lighting in its Philadelphia plant that opened a year ago. CEO Craig Yarde says peer pressure keeps people from abusing the napping privilege.

- Railroads such as the Burlington Northern Santa Fe Railway, based in Fort Worth, and the Omaha-based Union Pacific Railroad include napping as one element of a fatigue-management program. The industry has strict nap rules for engineers: naps are limited to layovers and cannot exceed forty-five minutes. The only problem, according to Union Pacific's director of alertness management: convincing workers it's OK to take a nap.

Overwhelming Cluelessness

Ron Lieber offers up some insights on the creativity that can accrue from a well-managed day, fresh eyes, and the entrepreneurial spirit. Many times, when your day is free of pressures, you can see the big picture and take advantage of opportunities. Consider these examples:

- Tom Scott of Nantucket Nectars believes the ability to achieve in the face of what can only be described as the "overwhelming cluelessness" most new entrepreneurs feel begins with a burning curiosity. "The thing that stuck with me from the first day was the rush, the fact that every day was something new.…And the more we picked up steam, the more that rush increased, because we realized we really could solve whatever problems came up."

• John Chuang started studying for an M.B.A. years after starting the staffing firm MacTemps. "Not only did I end up getting a lot out of the program, but the whole staff did, too," Chuang says, noting how he would come back to the office after class and tell his employees all about the tips he'd picked up that day.

• A truly unique product can sometimes sell itself while you learn about business as you go. Dave Kapell was a struggling heavy-metal guitarist with a quirky penchant for writing lyrics with words cut out from magazines. The idea stuck when he put words on magnets and stuck them on the fridge. Now, it seems every refrigerator in America has word squares on it, thanks to his company, Magnetic Poetry.

• Marcia Kilgore started Bliss, a wildly successful day spa in New York, even though the town was littered with similar businesses. "I never think about why something hasn't been done already; I think about why nobody has done it right yet."

• "There was never a point where I didn't think I could make it work," notes Todd Alexander, owner of Vendemmia, an Atlanta wine distributorship. "Ignorance is bliss. As long as I had a place to store the wine and a truck to deliver it in, I believed that, eventually, I would sell it at a profit."

- As a fashion editor, Kate Spade saw too many ugly, clunky handbags. So she teamed up with husband Andy to create the now-famous Kate Spade line of functional carryalls with clean lines and sharp colors. "We've seen the people in the newspapers who were laid off when they were fifty. We wanted to chase our own destiny." So they quit good jobs in 1993 to do just that, and sold about $30 million of product within five years.

- The ability to fall flat on your face and then peel yourself right off the pavement again takes a lot of self-confidence, something most young entrepreneurs have in spades. "Failure is part of the process," says Jason Olim, who started an online music retailer, CDNow, with his twin, Matthew. "Mistakes are the bricks with which you build businesses."[15]

TrendSmart Tip: Bear in mind that great time management makes you more creative, innovative, entrepreneurial— and a better manager. It frees you up to do what's *really* important in your business.

If I Had a Hammer...

Daniel Pink's excellent article on Michael Hammer's writings on time, speed, and process addresses other aspects of delayed urgencies.[16] "In the beginning (of the new economy)," he writes, "there was reengineering. And it was good. Then it was big. Then it got scary....Reengineering quickly became a synonym for firing lots of workers. *Fast Company* called it 'The Fad That Forgot People' in its inaugural issue in 1995," Pink writes.

Hammer sees it differently. Reengineering encompasses time management, speed to market, and cost-effective processes simultaneously.

"Financial measures—profitability, return on investment, discounted cash flow, or any of the technically complex measures used by financial engineers—tell you little, if anything, of what you need to know about your business," says Hammer. "The fundamental language of business is about work, not about money....The fundamental language of business is about things like customer satisfaction, speed, and error rates." Somewhere between Pink and Hammer, I find the real trend, wherein process engineering and many other such management models offer systems that identify and even codify the "important."

Hammer believes that processes within most companies "stink"—that companies are loose where they should be tight and tight where they should be loose. Hammer—a mathematician, an engineer, and, says Pink, "a man with a left brain the size of Wisconsin"—recognizes that further reengineering ultimately depends on qualities that emanate from the right side of the brain: devotion, trust, empathy, and all of their touchy-feely cousins.

Process reengineering requires consistent measurement at every step in order to isolate the "important" steps in any process. Measures that count include: How long does it take to turn around an application? What percentage of the time does a company deliver a product on the date the customer asks for? How many times a year does a firm turn its inventory? "Those are operating measures," says Pink, "metrics that matter not to the accounting department but to the all-powerful customer."

TrendSmart Tip: Know what is "important" to every step of every process in your company.

"Some people think reengineering means downsizing because some vulgar morons decided to apply it to their downsizing efforts because they were too embarrassed to call it downsizing," Hammer sermonizes. To him, reengineering "was never about reducing head count or throwing people out of work. It was—*it is*—simply the radical redesign of business processes for dramatic improvement."

"In my bible," Hammer says, "it only says that the love of *hand-offs* is the root of all evil!" And Hammer makes his point via a success story about an auto-parts company that took 140 days to get a sample to a customer until it changed its act. It eliminated waste. It reorganized activities. Sales and engineering began seeing clients together to grasp more clearly the clients' needs. The company began storing all of its previous designs on the engineers' workstations—which shrunk the design stage from three days to a few minutes. Instead of mailing the designs to the tooling plant, the engineers zapped them there electronically.

The list goes on. By reforming each stage, the auto-parts company had more time for refinements and revisions to suit the customer. The payoff was dramatic. The 140-day timeline shrunk to eighteen days. Overhead costs dropped by 50 percent. The company went from winning roughly one out of five bids to capturing four out of five.

From Scarce Goods to Scarce Customers

"Customers are no longer supplicants for scarce goods," Hammer writes in *The Agenda.* "Roles have changed, and sellers have become supplicants for scarce buyers." One example: today, the auto industry can produce nearly twenty million more vehicles a year than the world market demands.

This shift—from scarce goods to scarce customers—"is the essence of what will make the next decade of business different from previous ones," says Pink. "Customers want more for less—and they want it now."

But what about the employee, the one that "goes the extra mile"?

"It's not repeatable. It's not reliable. It's not dependable!" Hammer preaches. "It's episodic."

In Hammer's theology, the cardinal virtues are discipline, structure, and repeatability. Dogma plays a crucial role, too. There are, for Hammer, rights and wrongs, saints and sinners—especially where technology is involved. "The rise of the Internet is less important than the invention of air-conditioning," Hammer says. "What the Internet does is turbocharge phenomena that were already happening....It's more an extension of existing phenomena than something new....Nonetheless, the Web is a 'howitzer' for consumers....In the long run...the revolutionary impact of the Internet will be in dissolving boundaries between companies."

Disappearing Act

"The company as we know it will soon disappear," says Hammer. "The Last Big Thing was demolishing the walls within enterprises," he writes. "The Next Big Thing that will dominate business discourse for the coming decade is the destruction of walls between enterprises." Soon, he concludes, businesses will begin reengineering externally across enterprises.

Hammer calls this "virtual integration." Instead, for example, of sending yogurt to stores on separate trucks, competing companies may decide to share a truck. It makes sense, he says. "We're not competing on the cost of trucking. We're competing on the flavor of the yogurt, on its freshness, and on our advertising. If you and I share trucks, that's to the consumer's advantage."

When you ask people to make changes—large, frightening changes—you need to enlist not just their minds but also their hearts, and possibly their souls. In order to do that, the urgent is always delayed in favor of the important.

TrendSmart Tips

- Keep what's important at the forefront; look for the bigger picture; constantly prioritize and reprioritize.
- Do what's "urgent" only when what's really important is already done.
- Use time-management systems and software to help you achieve your goals and spend your time wisely.
- Bear in mind that great time management makes you more creative, innovative, entrepreneurial—and a better manager. It frees you up to do what's *really* important in your business.
- Know what is "important" to every step of every process in your company.

Chapter 5

Acrobatic Structures
Where Agility and Stability Meet

⊕ ⊕ ⊕

*"Let's take a walk, you
and I in spite of the
weather if it rains hard
on our toes."*
—Frank O'Hara, poet

The traditional boxes, silos, and arrows of organization charts are being replaced by dotted lines, images, and metaphors. Various observers of the positive changes in organizational structure now refer to them with euphemistic names such as spider webs, concentrics, donuts, galaxies, and constellations. Regardless of the terminology, *TrendSmart* leaders understand that the past thirty years have seen a shift in the basic nature of organizations toward being more flexible and responsive—to customers, to employees, and to shareholders. Organizations must withstand new pressures and strains and be capable of bending acrobatically.

TrendSmart Tip: To sustain success, organizations must withstand new pressures and strains and must be capable of bending acrobatically.

Managing the Boss

Fortunately, acrobatic structures have many good role models around the world. Lori Stacy tells of us of the maverick London ad agency St. Luke's Communications—an extremely acrobatic company. Among its clients, St. Luke's has the two largest advertising accounts in the UK—British Telecommunications and British Sky Broadcasting. But as atypical as St. Luke's is, it has "never had the funky client. I love the paradox," says CEO Andy Law.

Rather than the typical hierarchical corporate structure, at St. Luke's there are no bosses. The trustees of the Qualifying Employee Share Ownership Trust (Quest), a group of agency members voted upon each year by their peers, "manage" the organization. No one reports to Law or his partner, David Abraham; in fact, Law and Abraham report to the rest of the company.

At St. Luke's, says Stacy, "a new form of hierarchy is evolving—the hierarchy of persuasion," with those who have the most eloquence and logic being the ones most likely to be elected to serve as Quest trustees. "Culture is like the wind. It changes every time you add a new owner," says Law.

The only designated offices at St. Luke's belong to the clients. "There is a link between architecture/design and output," says Law, who, like each of the employees, can call just three things at St. Luke's offices his own—a cell phone, a locker, and a satchel. Law feels that the structure allows the group to use the building to help them work. "Here, you have to know what you're doing before you know where to go."

Creating the flexible structure and environment was not done in isolation. Law looks for inspiration to companies like Ericsson, IKEA, and Tata Steel of India, where the company's entire grounds are a conservation area and their employees are offered public education and private medical treatment. Among other things, Law credits these companies for "making human capital their most important asset, behind their products, and, even to an extent, their customers."

Oddly enough, for an agency revered for its treatment of employees, finding and hiring talent has become a huge challenge. At St. Luke's, there's no hiding behind power or a lofty title. Therefore, it takes a special kind of person to be comfortable in such an environment, and St. Luke's knows that their applicant talent pool is quite small.

Nonetheless, something about St. Luke's flair and style must be working—once people join, they want to stay. Since its inception, St. Luke's has had a turnover rate of just 10 percent. Factor out those who left the company for personal reasons, such as to raise a child or change careers, and the turnover rate drops to just 1 percent.[17]

When the Former Cannibalizes the Latter

Today's successful companies are nimble, agile, and flexible in their business plans, marketing strategies, brand development, and organizational structure. Shareholders, venture capitalists, strategic partners, and industry analysts have all come to see the inherent value in a deft, quick, pliable company. Today's executives in these companies know, as Andy Law does, that one of the newly rediscovered secret recipes for success is to mix equal parts of innovation and steady management.

TrendSmart Tip: Today's successful companies are nimble, agile, and flexible—in their business plans, marketing strategies, brand development, and organizational structure.

If nothing else, the implosion of so many dot-coms showed what can happen when the former (innovation) cannibalizes the latter (steady management)—when a good idea is left poorly managed or when good capital is thrown after a bad idea in search of a fast buck.

For the *TrendSmart* leader, striking a balance between innovation and steady management is a crucial skill. Knowing what to do is equally important as knowing what *not* to do. "There are plenty of books and articles about how to manage people," says an anonymously written letter to the editors of *Fast Company* magazine. "When are people going to realize that learning how *not* to manage employees is just as worthy a topic?"[18] Nowhere is this more pertinent than in understanding what to do and what not to do when managing today's increasingly complex, multigenerational workforce.

TrendSmart Tip: The implosion of so many dot-coms shows what can happen when innovation cannibalizes steady management (i.e., when a good idea is left poorly managed or when good capital is thrown after a bad idea in search of a fast buck).

Managing Multiple Generations

In the late 1990s, Lucent Technologies was the poster child of many innovative management practices. Though much has changed at Lucent—and some would say not for the better—the earlier lessons learned are still of value.

Phillip Britt describes the complex mix of long-term employees and new personnel at Lucent Technologies. Though the ranks are thinning, those managers and staff who were with AT&T prior to 1984, when it monopolized the phone industry, worked under a traditional style of management. The company structured hours and duties and left little room for employee input in company policies.

That all changed when Lucent got its own entity. Not only was the company free to make its own workplace rules, but it developed those rules in a manner to attract bright young engineers, who helped keep the company in the forefront of the competitive telecommunications industry. "Lucent is a very entrepreneurial company," says John Skalko, a Lucent human resources spokesman. "It's a very exciting, very diverse workplace environment." With a peak of 153,000 employees, Lucent's staffing was a microcosm of business today—young workers with different workplace values than those of older managers, and an increasing percentage of the workforce under thirty years of age.[19]

Though some businesses have more structured staffing needs, human-resource experts recommend that companies look at options such as flexible hours and telecommuting, as well as giving employees some leeway in how to accomplish their work. In fact, many benefits consultants recommend shifting to a focus on "outputs" (such as the number of files completed by data entry personnel) rather than "inputs" (the time a data entry worker actually spends on the job). *TrendSmart* leaders and managers do both.

Cows and Cowpokes

One good indication of a flexible company is its willingness to identify outdated practices, policies, and procedures—its "sacred cows"[20]—and to take steps to change with the times. In the fall of 1997, all 450 people in PBX pioneer Mitel's research and development division set off on what they refer to as a "sacred-cow hunt." Like good cowpokes, they vowed to round up every accepted practice that stood in the way of doing great work fast. Here are some examples of sacred cows and what the cowpokes did with them:

- **Sacred cow:** *Twice is nice.* People in the testing department routinely duplicated tests already performed by their colleagues in the design and engineering departments.
- **The cowpoke:** *Once is enough.* Mitel now has a "one test" policy that has shaved an entire week off the average product-development time.

- **Sacred cow:** *It's not my problem.* Departments within research and development used to butt heads more often than they swapped ideas. Once, for example, a customer reported that a Mitel phone system was randomly disconnecting as many as thirty phone calls at a time. A support technician believed that the glitch was software related. When he shared this theory with the system's designer, he was told to "prove it." Eventually he did, and the designer fixed the glitch—but only after the customer suffered for nineteen weeks!
- **The cowpoke:** *It's everyone's problem.* "Now, when product support asks for help, people focus on fixing the problem rather than finding fault," says Geoff Smith, 46, Mitel's research and development chief.

- **Sacred cow:** *Take your time.* Every product-development plan has deadlines. Before the sacred-cow hunts, stretching them was an accepted way of doing business at Mitel.
- **The cowpoke:** *On time, all the time.* Mitel's research and development group will do whatever it takes to move faster. Recently, for example, a manager learned that the manufacturing division didn't have enough workers to ship an important new product on time. So he paid secretaries to stay late and work the production line.[21]

One of the most common sacred cows is the longstanding practice in many companies of filling full-time vacancies with full-time employees. In recent years, with the growth and sophistication of the interim staffing industry, many savvy companies now utilize a flexible workforce on a just-in-time, as-needed basis. Talented writer Daniel Pink offers useful insight into the world of temporary and interim workers.[22]

TrendSmart Tip: One good indication of a flexible company is its willingness to identify outdated practices, policies, and procedures—its "sacred cows"— and to take steps to change with the times.

Be Acrobatic When Hiring Human Capital

Pink looks at MacTemps, which, he says, "is perhaps the most robust and fully articulated example of a company that's reckoning with a world in which human capital functions like financial capital." Three things set it apart from the temp-agency pack:

- *First: Think NASDAQ.* Individuals must qualify to be "listed" on the MacTemps exchange—a process that involves written tests, computer simulations, two intense interviews, a careful analysis of past work performance, and an assessment of likely future work performance. Just 10 percent of all applicants who go through the interview and testing process end up meeting the agency standard; the rest lack either the know-how, the track record, or the personality to make it as a MacTemps free agent.
- *Second: Think talent agency.* "Think Jerry Maguire," says Aimee Youngblood, 28, an assignment manager at MacTemps in Dallas. "I help them help me help them. I

help them find assignments. I manage their careers."

- *Third: Think HR department.* MacTemps offers you health insurance, a 401(k) plan, even vacation pay. If you get work through MacTemps, you don't have to worry about wrestling your paycheck from a slow-paying client. MacTemps does that dirty work for you—and pays you on time. Nor do you have to keep track of your 1099s or pay quarterly estimated taxes. MacTemps gives you a W-2— not a 1099—and withholds the taxes for you.

Find a Corporate *Yenta* to Solve Your Staffing Needs

Pink also looks at one of my favorite companies, San Francisco's M^2, an interim staffing agency specializing in high-level "executive consultants." I'm especially familiar with M^2, having referred M^2 consultants to many of my clients and more recently serving on its corporate board of directors, Logical Options of South Africa. Recently, I had the opportunity to interact with a large number of M^2 consultants.

In San Francisco's financial district, in pursuit of some "good lucky" (see chapter 8), dozens of people fill a room to hear me speak, at the invitation of my friend M^2 cofounder Paula Reynolds. It matters little that it is nearly 7 P.M., as all in the room look crisp, sharp, and professional. They come to hear me speak on leadership and innovation to some extent, but I know full well that if they are smart, the real reason to attend is to mingle and schmooze and get some face-to-face time with Paula, to raise her awareness of them amongst the M^2 network of more than eight thousand consultants. The opportunity to network and gather leads is at the top of their minds. The fact that they give me a hearty round of applause and that everyone present gets a copy of my last book is icing on my cake. Their "real" icing comes not from having my book, but introductions and follow-up to the evening meeting.

M² consultants master the networking game and in so doing provide M² with a seasoned and talented labor pool. In this sense, the consultants contribute to a win-win situation wherein M² can provide invaluable, specialized services to corporate clients. M² "gives new meaning to old terms by playing the talent game by new rules," says Pink. "Like MacTemps, it connects buyers of free-agent talent with sellers of free-agent talent, a kind of corporate *yenta*. Its goal is to achieve a perfect match."

Pink quotes cofounder and CEO Marion McGovern, who calls the company "an arbitrageur of talent." In other words, it profits from price discrepancies between different markets. It "purchases" talent at a price that sellers are willing to accept—and then "sells" the talent to buyers willing to pay a higher price. In M²'s case, a 30 to 35 percent markup on its talent yields revenue of millions of dollars yearly.

So adept is McGovern at the interim staffing game that she has literally written the book on it, *A New Brand of Expertise*.[23] "But her vision was not without its detractors," says Pink. "In 1988, when McGovern launched the company with Reynolds, the terms 'talent market' and 'human capital' were not found in the conventional business vocabulary. But McGovern knew she had to educate in order to sell the services of M². A dozen years later, M² attracts the best of the best, free-lancers with in-depth experience. The minimum requirements: at least ten years of work experience; not seeking a full time job; good people skills; and demonstrated success in previous jobs and assignments. Even though M² does very little advertising, about fifty new applicants approach the company each week."

Claire McAuliffe, the third of M²'s three principals, describes the company as a flexible hybrid: "We're not a search firm. We're not a consulting firm. We're not a temp agency. We're not a dating service.

We're sort of…an honest broker who works to make the matches that make the talent market work." The company bills itself as "the premier broker of independent consultants to companies in need of 'spot-market' expertise and just-in-time management staffing."

The good news for companies is that a wide array of new resources to provide solutions for staffing issues has emerged. Companies such as MacTemps and M² are but two examples of a much broader resource base.

A Bright IDEO

Palo Alto–based IDEO, much like M², is a broker and hybrid too, working with a wide range of clients from many, many industries to turn clients' ideas into products and designs. For example, IDEO designed the basic computer mouse that has become the industry standard. On a recent edition of the U.S. television show *Dateline*, within one week, with cameras rolling, IDEO came up with a new design for a better grocery cart.

To execute this kind of product development so quickly requires an acrobatic structure that supports the acrobatic minds IDEO hires. When I last visited them, they had several scattered locations within a few blocks of the Stanford University campus. IDEO made use of everything from old office space to a gutted auto repair shop. Each office had its own character, whimsy, and décor, comfortable spaces where people were obviously free to create and were still highly professional and productive—a good blend of attributes in any company.

Another acrobatic company with a big idea, IKEA, has grown and become profitable by implementing a few simple ideas: making well-designed furniture and home products available at a reasonable price, to a worldwide customer base (I also discuss IKEA in chapter 11). To accomplish this, IKEA used some acrobatic rethinking that challenged industry conventions. It reconfigured the standard retail showroom, transforming it from a hodgepodge of disparate offerings (couches over here, lighting over there, rugs out in the back) to an array of rooms that display the possible *combinations* of IKEA products (a room with one couch, one light, and one rug shown together). Instead of leasing dozens and dozens of small showrooms, IKEA opted for showrooms larger than soccer stadiums.

Temptations of the CEO

Not all business concepts are as nimble as these all-caps companies, IDEO and IKEA. Certainly, the long drama of ups and downs of other all-cappers (e.g., IBM and GE), is well chronicled. In working with presidents and CEOs of complex multinational corporations, I observe how often a company's performance reflects its leaders. Nimble companies mirror nimble leaders; low-performing companies, unfortunately, resemble their leadership as well.

My colleague Pat Lencioni, president of The Table Group in Emeryville, California, and author of *The Five Temptations of a CEO*,[24] has studied CEOs in depth and has identified some of their common shortcomings. Business writer Dave Murphy summarizes them for us:

- *Choosing invulnerability over trust:* CEOs with low self-esteem are afraid to appear vulnerable and are overly concerned with appearing powerful. Thus, they resist being challenged and tend to hire inferior workers who won't pose a threat.
- *Discouraging conflict:* CEOs who are uncomfortable with conflict discourage it among managers and in meetings. They also aren't likely to hire innovative talent.

• *Being too afraid of having to change a decision:* Afraid of looking bad, some CEOs avoid making decisions until they have more information and fear changing course later, succumbing to the proverbial "paralysis by analysis."

• *Being more concerned about popularity than accountability:* Weak CEOs avoid giving negative feedback to employees. They prefer firing people to telling them the truth about their performance and jeopardizing their own popularity. Compounding this, in the absence of such feedback, they fail to make clear what their expectations are, leaving their staff to second guess.

• *Being more interested in protecting their status than achieving results:* Some CEOs are so enamored of the title that they are more concerned with enhancing their own reputation than that of the company.[25]

On the flip side of these temptations are necessary skills that *TrendSmart* leaders today need to effect productivity and profitability. Exhibit 5-1 provides details.

Exhibit 5-1. Of M-I-C-E and Men

TrendSmart leaders today will have to overcome their insecurities and make a conscious effort to master four cornerstone skills that affect productivity and profitability. I refer to these skills with the acronym "MICE," and offer the following working definitions from a business perspective:

• Motivation: a force, vision, or belief that influences a person's inner drive and outward behavior.
• Innovation: the act of creating and implementing new

ideas, processes, products, or technologies.

• Communication: the mutual exchange of information, emotions, ideas, and/or expectations between individuals and/or between individuals and organizations.

• Evaluation: an accurate examination of a person's skills and effectiveness in meeting personal, professional, and/or organizational goals and expectations.

Mastery of these four skills can make an ordinary CEO, or any manager for that matter, into an extraordinary leader. To be able to effectively motivate, innovate, communicate, and evaluate is where the science of management and leadership becomes an art form.

TrendSmart Tip: Be flexible and understand the resources available to you. Motivate, innovate, communicate, and evaluate.

Who Hurled the Rock at the Glass Ceiling?

In my experience, flexible companies with acrobatic structures are disproportionately headed by women. Unfortunately, for women to have access to the highest positions in a company, the support and mentoring of their male colleagues is often required. Consider the following example from Hewlett-Packard's recent history.

"With more than a quarter of Hewlett-Packard's managers women," writes Reed Abelson, "it seemed incontestable that the glass ceiling that stops the rise of female executives at so many other companies had been shattered. But who hurled the rock?"

"The surprising answer," says Abelson, "a middle-aged white guy," former HP chairman, Lewis E. Platt. Like most fast-track male executives, Platt never thought much about women in the workplace—until he was thrust suddenly into the challenging role of single parent after his wife died of cancer. Suddenly, he had to make dinner for his two daughters, get them to school, make sure they did their homework in the evenings, and even find the time to go grocery shopping.

Named a vice president, Platt continued his ascent at Hewlett-Packard, managing various parts of the company's computer business, and ultimately becoming CEO, replacing John Young. During his tenure, more women were rising to the level of manager, but few were making it to the highest ranks. With his new perspective, Platt set out to change this.

While many companies offer flexible schedules and job sharing to accommodate employees with families, few corporations actually encourage their use. Hewlett-Packard did. Platt made speeches, reminding managers that they needed to consider seriously any of their employees' requests to take advantage of this new flexibility, and he put his name on memos sent to managers across the world. "Work-life issues are a business priority," one statement said. It is not surprising, then, that when Platt retired as CEO, he enthusiastically supported the naming of his replacement, Carly Fiorina.[26]

In this case, Platt not only "did the right thing"; it made good business sense. "Attention to work-life issues strengthens HP's competitive edge and improves teamwork within HP," says Platt. The company says it loses fewer than 5 percent of its employees each year, compared with an industry average that consulting firm William M. Mercer puts at 17 percent.

Nothing in Nature Retires

Male or female, leaders who wish to expand their MICE skill-set have to boldly step out, take some risks, and stave off complacency if they wish to remain flexible and quick. *TrendSmart* "fast" companies change quickly, are structurally acrobatic, have a mix of "adults" in the recipe, and think strategically. They can "connect the dots" of the marketplace until a picture forms.

When *TrendSmart* leaders see the picture that has formed, they place earlier difficulties in perspective. For example, most businesses confuse their strengths and their core competencies. A strength is usually not a core competency. A core competency helps give you the competitive advantage, especially when many competitors share similar strengths. A core competency, therefore, is a *distinguishing and differentiating* strength, one that others cannot match at a given point in time. Therefore, strengths are many, core competencies few.

Some leaders run their business according to the motto "Under-promise and overdeliver." To me, that is a sure recipe for mediocrity. At the very least, promise what you can deliver, and push to exceed that as often as possible.

To dominate your market in today's economy, you have to dare to be first. First to see trends. First to market. First to anticipate change. First to admit when you make a mistake. First to not rest on past success.

Also, you can dominate by running with someone else's idea and being better at it. Oftentimes, number two becomes number one. The idea can be another's, but the execution of the idea may be your value-add. Many of our best-known brands, like Coca-Cola or Nike, were not the inventors of the products they are now synonymous with. The ideas of soda and sneakers well preceded them. If I see a good idea, I will beg, borrow, or steal it! I do not have to have invented it; all I have to do is know a good idea when I see one. The point is to keep your eyes open to everything and everybody.

TrendSmart Tip: Dare to be first. First to see trends. First to market. First to anticipate change. First to admit when you make a mistake. First to not rest on past success.

You must also take risks if you want to *stay* in business. My mom used to say, "Nothing in nature retires." I believe that is true in business, too. Today, there are only the consistently quick…and the prematurely dead.

Finally, to energize the creativity in a company, *TrendSmart* leaders should start by getting to know employees, customers, and shareholders. Then, they need to build a relationship with them and see the interrelationship between all of them. Savvy leaders need to understand all three—customers, employees, and investors—especially in a fickle world.

TrendSmart **Tips**

- To sustain success, organizations must withstand new pressures and strains and must be capable of bending acrobatically.
- Today's successful companies are nimble, agile, and flexible—in their business plans, marketing strategies, brand development, and organizational structure.
- The implosion of so many dot-coms shows what can happen when innovation cannibalizes steady management (i.e., when a good idea is left poorly managed or when good capital is thrown after a bad idea in search of a fast buck).
- One good indication of a flexible company is its willingness to identify outdated practices, policies, and procedures—its "sacred cows"—and to take steps to change with the times.
- Be flexible and understand the resources available to you. Motivate, innovate, communicate, and evaluate.
- Dare to be first. First to see trends. First to market. First to anticipate change. First to admit when you make a mistake. First to not rest on past success.

Chapter 6

Grounded Risks
Where Bold Action Aligns with Bold Values

⊕ ⊕ ⊕

"Confusion arises when we assume
the symbol stands for something."
—*Joanne Kyger,* Japan and India Journals

I make a distinction between taking risks and taking chances. Conventional wisdom tends to confuse the two concepts, and it is important to understand the differences. Taking *risks* is based upon three steps:

1. Prepare.
2. Prepare some more.
3. Prepare again.

Taking *chances,* on the other hand, involves plunging into a situation unprepared:

1. See the diving board.
2. Jump off the edge.
3. Live (or die) with the results.

When you don't do your homework, you may be unpleasantly surprised to find that the pool was drained the day before!

TrendSmart Tip: Taking risks is different from taking chances: risk taking is based on *being prepared*.

Today, more than ever, *TrendSmart* managers seize opportunities to take risks based on objective inquiry, strong intuition, prior experience, educated estimates, and what-if analysis. But they are not comfortable taking chances, especially those that involve high levels of unidentified uncertainty and haphazard, impulsive action—the proverbial roll of the dice.

My colleague and friend Ken Beller, president of Near Bridge, Inc., exemplifies the union of bold business action and strong personal values. He has led new corporate ventures, implemented exponential change, and accelerated dynamic growth at companies such as General Electric, DaimlerChrysler, and Etec Systems (an Applied Materials Company). In his leadership style are the attributes of all leaders today. His values provide a grounding for the risks he takes.

TrendSmart Tip: Seize opportunities to take risks based on objective inquiry, strong intuition, prior experience, educated estimates, and what-if analysis.

What Risk Takers Know

TrendSmart leaders leave nothing to chance. For example, after many years of iffy funding, venture capitalists on Sand Hill Road in Palo Alto, California, now place a higher value than ever on management abilities and the business model rather than on "the next great—but not implementable—idea," as one venture-capital partner told me. A good venture capitalist knows that these days the path to profitability passes through the gate of experience.

Risk takers have several skills in common. They know:

- How to build on strengths and minimize liabilities in order to take the riskiness out of risk.
- How to overcome firehosing (the knee-jerk dousing of ideas in ourselves and others) and take enough risk to find the extraordinary in the ordinary.
- How to be team players—surrounding themselves with others, bringing out the "star quality" in one another, creating a team that outperforms and is greater than the sum of the individual players—thereby creating a nurturing, supportive framework that encourages the team to take the necessary risks.
- How to find balance in order to perform at their best, day in and day out, when everything—and *nothing*—is on the line, until risk taking is a normal part of life.
- How to kindle the fire in their hearts and share contagious enthusiasm, which gives the people the dreams and the passion to make them *want* to risk enough to make those dreams come true.
- How to learn from mistakes—from those occasions where they did not risk enough—as well as situations where they

did take the risks needed to be successful.

• How to match risk and reward. In the words of John F. Kennedy, "There are risks and costs to a program of action, but they are far less than the long-range risks and costs of comfortable inaction." The irony is that often the rewards far exceed the risk itself.

Two Views from the Top

I have often seen the truth in the Zen adage that many paths can lead to the top of the mountain. Two of America's richest men, though respectful of each other, have dramatically differing views on numbers specifically and investing in general. Yet both have been very successful by taking risks of a certain—but very different—kind.

As the twentieth century drew to a close, Bill Gates and Warren Buffett gave a very special lecture for 350 business-school students and a few lucky guests at the University of Washington. These two business icons amicably engaged in a dialogue that revealed some similarities and a world of differences. What follows is a summary of the dialogue as reported in *Fortune.*[27]

On horsepower:

Buffett: "I always look at IQ and talent as representing the horsepower of the motor, but that the output—the efficiency with which that motor works—depends on rationality."

Gates: "By pursuing software with a pretty incredible focus and by being there at the very beginning of the industry, we were able to build a company that has played a very central role in what's been a pretty big revolution."

On success:

Buffett: "I'd advise you that when you go out to work, work for an organization of people you admire, because it will turn you on."

Gates: "For me, that's working with very smart people and it's working on new problems."

On innovation:

Buffett: "At least three-quarters of the managers that we have are rich beyond any possible financial need, and therefore my job is to help my senior people keep them interested enough to want to jump out of bed at six o'clock in the morning and work with all of the enthusiasm they did when they were poor and starting."

Gates: "A company like ours has to attract a lot of people who think in different ways, it has to allow a lot of dissent, and then it has to recognize the right ideas and put some real energy behind them."

On change, or the absence thereof:

Buffett: "I look for businesses in which I think I can predict what they're going to look like in ten or fifteen or twenty years. So I focus on an absence of change."

Gates: "There will be this shift where, instead of your income level being determined by what country you are from, it will be determined by your education level."

On wisdom and advice:

Gates: "You have to be careful, if you're good at something, to make sure you don't think you're good at other things that you aren't necessarily so good at."

Buffett: "I'm very suspect of the person who is very good at one business who starts thinking they should tell the world how to behave on everything. For us to think that just because we made a lot of money, we're going to be better at giving advice on every subject—well, that's just crazy."

There you have it. Two different views, two different strategic minds. By quoting them, I hope I have given you a glimpse of their minds at work. Each remains focused on, even loyal to, his strategies.

Plan for Your Success...Backward!

In Buffett and Gates we see two different styles—two different approaches to risk. But the common denominator is that both have taken and will continue to take risks. You can too.

Think of a decision that you have been putting off because the outcome was unclear. You can learn how to prepare yourself for several possible outcomes by previewing possible scenarios. Then you can learn how to shift from "can't do" to "can do" thinking. Learning these skills helps you minimize the chance factors and maximize the calculated risk, the yield, and the potential for success.

One of the skills I use all the time is something I call "backcasting." Whereas forecasting examines the present in light of the past and projects the past into the future, backcasting assumes a successful future outcome. In backcasting, you select the best scenario—your dreams and visions for yourself or your company in the future—and you work *back* from that point to the present. You assume the outcome has come to pass—say, in the next five years—and you create an action plan for yourself in which you determine what risks you had to take and in what sequence. This best-case scenario then becomes your destination. With your successful future now identified, you begin by enthusiastically moving...backward.

TrendSmart Tip: Combine hunches with appropriate due diligence and research, and powerful initiatives will arise.

Using backcasting, our fears and passions become our allies. With backcasting, you can identify variables and forces that may affect future success. Then you can readily see which internal forces are within your control and which are not. By harnessing the internal forces—those things that you can control—you increase the odds of success. As the great Greek historian Herodotus expressed, "Great deeds are usually wrought at great risks."

Learning from History's BIG Risks

There are times when a series of small risks is all we have to face. Once in a while, however, we can take solace and gain encouragement by examining some really, really big risks that were taken in other eras. To Ken Beller, "all great achievements start with a dream or goal that seems absurd at the time. For example, who in their right mind would have ever thought about splitting a continent into two by digging the Panama Canal?"

Beller describes the massive scale of the original dream to give a sense of the proportions of the risk. To give me some perspective on the monumental efforts of these projects, he shared with me some interesting facts on the construction of the Panama Canal:

- The digging of the canal was begun in 1880 by Ferdinand de Lesseps, the French engineer who built the Suez Canal, and was completed thirty-four years later in 1914 by the United States.
- More than eighty thousand people took part in the construction of the canal; thirty thousand lost their lives.
- The project cost $639 million at the time—$11.8 billion in today's dollars.

After the Panama Canal was completed, ships traveling from New York to San Francisco no longer had to travel around South America, thereby saving 7,872 miles. Ferdinand de Lesseps's big dream and bigger risk literally changed the nature of international commerce for several decades.

When I asked Ken Beller what lessons he learned from the story of the building of the Panama Canal, he said, "The real key to leading and implementing revolutionary changes starts with recognizing that the only constant in life is change. Once this becomes part of your being, you can determine what to change and how to go about doing it. Unfortunately, most people and businesses still think that rearranging the deck chairs on the *Titanic* is an example of change. *Real* change takes innovative, out-of-the-box thinking. You have to be able to dream and dream big if you ever want to break the mold you are currently stuck in. If you always do what you've always done, you'll always get what you've always gotten."

Strategy and Risk Taking Guided by Intuition

Strategy, like electricity, is much easier to measure than to define. We can see the outcomes of good strategy in EBITDA (Earnings Before Interest, Taxes, Depreciation, and Amortization), percentage increases in sales and revenues, productivity ratios, and many more numerical indicators. This said, I hasten to add that in my twenty years in the strategy arena, there have been countless occasions where the "best" strategies—the ones that yield positive, even exponential numbers—have, truth be told, been decided upon through very subjective means. A CEO "just has a hunch," or a company president "can feel it in her bones." Combine the hunch with appropriate due diligence and research, and powerful strategic initiatives arise, often out of the ashes.

In the Zulu language, the harmonious musical and dance style performed by Ladysmith Black Mambazo is called "isicathimiya." The word means "tiptoe guys," according to leader Joseph Shabalala.[28] The term could easily apply to many a major decision made in corporate boardrooms, where the members tiptoe around the numbers trying to divine their next strategic move. These days, there is value in trusting both the numbers and reasoned intuition. The careful use of intuitive numbers, therefore, is a powerful means to sustainable success.

TrendSmart Tip: Part of the entrepreneurial spirit is the ability to take risks, follow a dream or vision, and make the strategic first moves well *before* all the numbers are in place to support the endeavor.

For example, on a recent trip to London I spent some time with an executive vice president for the Standard Bank of South Africa. I asked him about large merchant banking decisions, where perhaps billions of investment dollars rest on good judgment. He told me of situations where he and his colleagues sit in a room, analyze the objective numbers before them, and accept or reject a proposal "in spite of the numbers," pro or con.

Part of what is normally understood to be the entrepreneurial spirit, which I will discuss at many points in this book, is the ability to take risks, follow a dream or vision, and make the strategic first moves well *before* all the numbers are in place to support the endeavor.

Entrepreneurs love to take risks, so it's no surprise, for example, that an inordinate number of *Inc 500* CEOs are also pilots.[29] Kevin Heronimus of Advanced Composites Technology even dropped out of an M.B.A. program to build his own plane. But when it came time to secure a line of credit for his company, Heronimus proudly offered the $70,000 plane as collateral. He still has the plane, along with two others, which he and his staff use to visit the company's one hundred franchisees. Heronimus has even taken to hiring staff based on their flying skills. "I got one flyboy right out of the Navy," he says. "He's also an electrical engineer and our Internet expert. How's that for a find?"

TrendSmart leaders are also able to take the initiative quickly, so when they see an emerging trend or pattern, they take action. They have little tolerance or respect for those who rely on "the paralysis of analysis."

TrendSmart Tip: Take initiative quickly; when you see an emerging trend or pattern, take action.

Mirror, Mirror: Who's the Smartest of Them All?

One sure cure for paralysis by analysis is to learn from experience. "The difference between being smart and being wise is that smart people learn from their own mistakes," says George Gendron, "whereas wise people learn from the mistakes of *others*."[30] I'd add a corollary—namely, that the wisest people learn from smart people's mistakes. Why? Because smart people tend to make more interesting mistakes than the rest of us do—mistakes that reveal something not just about the perpetrator's foibles but also about the world at large. Further, most mistakes in business occur in relative obscurity and privacy.

TrendSmart Tip: Learn from smart people's mistakes.

Things could be worse. Suppose your errors were counted and published every day, like those of baseball players. Or suppose you ran a business as Babe Ruth once described his hitting: "I swing big, with everything I've got. I hit big or I miss big. I like to live as big as I can." Or, as director Joseph Mankiewicz says, "The difference between life and the movies is that a script has to make sense and life doesn't."

Consider too how "going by the book" and then by the numbers can lead you away from greater and long-term profitability. John Koss, chairman of the Milwaukee-based Koss Corp., which recently celebrated the 40th anniversary of the invention of the stereo headphone, speaks of customer reaction: "They would just go nuts with the phones, because you've got to remember that this was something that was never heard before."[31]

Bolstered by early success, and using accepted econometric and business measures, Koss diversified into other consumer electronics, with poor results. In the 1960s, Koss bought a maker of manual turntables—just as automatic record changers were taking over the market. In the 1980s, the company tried to take on Sony's Walkman and ended up millions in debt. Koss, which had been publicly traded since 1966, eventually filed for Chapter 11 bankruptcy protection.

"We didn't diversify, we 'deworsified' the business," Michael Koss, president and CEO, says in hindsight.

You Are What You Value

The sociologist C. Wright Mills once observed that organizations are always a reflection of both personal biography and organizational history. Companies, he understood, are not abstractions, but rather are more properly understood as a configuration of personal biographies at work at any point in time. Guided by Mills's insight, I have seen the relationship between individual values, the actions people take, and the profitability of an enterprise. Good people with good values make good companies.

As Ken Beller told me, paraphrasing the eminent American anthropologist Margaret Mead, "If we are to achieve a richer culture, rich in contrasting values, we must recognize the whole gamut of human potentialities, and so weave a less arbitrary social fabric, one in which each diverse human gift will find a fitting place."

For decades, there has been a marked separation between "who you are" and "what you do" for a living. In other words, for many people, their personal identity is not synonymous with the work they do. A flight attendant may be involved with million-dollar fund-raising campaigns in the local arts, a carpenter may paint exquisite murals, and a programmer may be the national spokesperson for an animal-rights organization.

This said, one emerging trend is the intentional effort by companies to understand personal values and to align personal core values with the core values of a company. When this is done, the gap between who you are and what you do diminishes greatly.

Managing in an environment of aligned personal and company

values is a delicate but very rewarding endeavor because work gets "personal" at times. *TrendSmart* managers have to be inherently practical, yet still understand that value-based management has more emotional content than the norm.

Aligning Personal and Workplace Values

Southwest Airlines is a good example of a place where personal and workplace values are closely aligned. At Southwest, a high premium is placed on the zany mixture of profitability and fun. Persons with no sense of humor and no work ethic need not apply. Its flight attendants are friendly and efficient, wear casual clothing, and joke throughout the flight. They are encouraged to personalize their safety messages, thereby capturing the attention of passengers. Staff at the boarding gates often decorate their stations in line with a new promotion or season.

Southwest's clear and simple core values help it to reap rewards, including the ability to attract and retain a talented workforce and, according to the U.S. Bureau of Transportation Statistics, the frequent distinction of No. 1 on-time carrier in the nation.

Another value at Southwest is uniqueness. As a company, from its inception, it never played by the rules of the "airline game." A maverick from the beginning, it focused on creating a better airline, not on beating the competition. One key to Southwest's success has been its ability to turn its back on the competition and thereby create its own playing field.

By acting on its own vision and values, Southwest avoided many common pitfalls of those who compete, including:

- Competition breeds conformity of goals and plans.
- Competition leads to imitation of others.
- Watching the competition discourages significant innovation.
- Competing at someone else's game is a reactionary strategy.

Law's Laws

Another interesting model of the link between bold actions, bold values, and taking grounded risks is the London ad agency St. Luke's Communications, also discussed in chapter 5. Committed to total equal employee ownership and the pursuit of personal values, St. Luke's has challenged almost every preconceived notion of how modern work should be done. St. Luke's chairman, Andy Law, wrote a book called *Creative Company,* which outlines Law's law: eclectic preparatory hints for taking risks and for separating yourself from the competition, summarized in Exhibit 6-1.

Exhibit 6-1. Andy Law's Bold Strategic Vision

1. Ask yourself what you want out of life.
2. Ask yourself what really matters to you.
3. Wear what you feel is really you.
4. Talk to people (even those you don't like) about 1 and 2. ("You should be feeling very uncomfortable now. You may even be sick. This is normal," says Law.)
5. Give up something you think you need most at work (desk, company car, etc.).
6. Trust everyone you meet. Keep every agreement you make. ("You should be feeling a little better now," he quips.)
7. Enjoy an exciting group experience (parachuting, kayaking).
8. Rewrite your business plan to align all of the above with your customers.
9. Draw a line on the office floor and invite everyone to enter a brave new world.
10. Share everything you do and own fairly with everyone who crosses the line. ("You should be feeling liberated.

> Soon you will have, in this order, the following: grateful customers, inspired employees, friendly communities, money.")[32]

There is value to offering "laws" based on values in any company because they provide building blocks for future success. Laying down the laws also helps put St. Luke's way ahead of the competition, especially if the competition tries to reconfigure their companies according to Law's laws, rather than creating their own. By the time the competition figures it out, Andy will have other laws and be even farther ahead of the game.

Who You Lead, What You Manage

Ken Beller, with his extensive experience in operations, has a law of his own: "You lead people; you manage inventory." Credible leadership is established by values lived out, not rules or positions of authority. Once values are aligned across a diagonal slice of a company's operations—from customer to CEO to newest employee—bold values will foster bold actions.

Values drive actions internally, without external monitoring and prodding. Value-based "carrots" are replacing rule-based "sticks," and risk is replacing chance as the staple of the culture. When values are the basis of action, profitability is greatly enhanced. When values are measured, *TrendSmart* leaders are able to establish goals and empower people to perform to set expectations. Give them the resources they need, and get out of the way!

TrendSmart Tip: Bold values will foster bold actions.

TrendSmart **Tips**

- Taking risks is different from taking chances: risk taking is based on *being prepared*.
- Seize opportunities to take risks based on objective inquiry, strong intuition, prior experience, educated estimates, and what-if analysis.
- Combine hunches with appropriate due diligence and research, and powerful initiatives will arise.
- Part of the entrepreneurial spirit is the ability to take risks, follow a dream or vision, and make the strategic first moves well *before* all the numbers are in place to support the endeavor.
- Take initiative quickly; when you see an emerging trend or pattern, take action.
- Learn from smart people's mistakes.
- Bold values will foster bold actions.

Chapter 7

Standard Deviations

Where the Creative Exception Becomes the Norm

⊕ ⊕ ⊕

"The 'duende'…rejects all sweet geometry one has learned…
it breaks with all styles…"

—*Federico García Lorca*

TrendSmart leaders are creative, and creative people operate on the far edges of the Gaussian bell curve, a discernible "standard deviation" from the norm, to borrow a term from statisticians. In fact, they seek to make deviating from the norm the standard, the expected. Operating outside the realm of logic and deductive thinking, they are adept at making surprising associations and seeing things differently. "If they look at research, new technology, or trends, they can piece those together and draw a mosaic and end up with something completely different," says Thomas Kuczmarski, a

Chicago-based consultant who specializes in innovation.[33]

Creativity is much more than the delegated pursuit of novelty. In many companies, creativity is considered to be the exclusive domain and responsibility of the "creative people." I always have to chuckle when, for example, an ad agency—an inherently creative endeavor—has a "creative department." There is a little bit of creativity in all of us, and an equal reticence to show it.

TrendSmart Tip: Make deviating from the norm the standard, the expected. Think of this as a new kind of "standard deviation."

The Ruts of Logic

Habits and logic make for some odd outcomes. Without consciously looking for creative solutions, most of us are not able to see things differently. The following story illustrates this humorously.

The U.S. standard railroad gauge (distance between the rails) is 4 feet, 8.5 inches. That is an exceedingly odd number. Why was that gauge used? Because that's the way they built them in England, and the U.S. railroads were built by English expatriates. Why did the English build them that way? Because the first rail lines were built by the same people who built the pre-railroad tramways, and that's the gauge they used. Why did "they" use that gauge? Because the people who built the tramway used the same jigs and tools that they used for building wagons, which used that wheel spacing.

So why did the wagons have that particular odd spacing? Well, if they tried to use any other spacing, the wagon wheels would break on some of the old, long-distance roads in England because that was the spacing of the wheel ruts.

So who built those old, rutted roads? The first long-distance roads in Europe (and England) were built by Imperial Rome for their legions.

The roads have been used ever since. And the ruts in the roads? The ruts in the roads, which everyone had to match for fear of destroying their wagon wheels, were first formed by Roman war chariots. Since the chariots were made for (or by) Imperial Rome, they were all alike in the matter of wheel spacing. The U.S. standard railroad gauge of 4 feet, 8.5 inches derives from the original specification for an Imperial Roman war chariot. Specifications and bureaucracies live forever.

So the next time you are handed a specification and wonder what horse's behind came up with it, you may be exactly right, because the Imperial Roman war chariots were made just wide enough to accommodate the back end of two war horses. Thus we have the answer to the original question.

Now for the twist to the story. When we see a space shuttle sitting on its launching pad, there are two booster rockets attached to the side of the main fuel tank. These are solid rocket boosters, or SRBs. The SRBs are made by Thiokol at its factory in Utah. The engineers who designed the SRBs might have preferred to make them a bit fatter, but the SRBs had to be shipped by train from the factory to the launch site. The railroad line from the factory had to run through a tunnel in the mountains. The tunnel is slightly wider than the railroad track, and the railroad track is about as wide as two horses' rumps. So, a major design feature of what is arguably the world's most advanced transportation system, a space shuttle, was determined more than two thousand years ago by the width of a horse's hindquarters!

Don't you just love logic?

Disruptive Innovations

Creativity is a necessary first step in the process of innovation, which culminates in the implementation of ideas. "Having ideas and creating [inventions] isn't sufficient," says John Seely Brown, Xerox's chief scientist. "We have to move from invention to innovation, which means finding ways to implement our inventions."[34] Innovation is complex and can serve multiple purposes.

Clayton Christensen makes an important distinction between sustaining and disruptive innovations: *Sustaining innovations* are ideas that enable market leaders in a given industry to serve their customers better. *Disruptive innovations*, ironically, are technologies or business models that do a "worse" job or contain fewer features than the existing products—and yet they open up whole new markets.

Christensen gives the example of Intuit. "When Intuit introduced QuickBooks, a smaller, cheaper program with far less functionality [than competing accounting software packages], the existing market leaders responded by adding still more features and expense to their programs. That may have kept their own customers happy," he says, "but it ignored the much larger market of customers who needed only what QuickBooks offered." The result was that QuickBooks captured 70 percent of the small-business accounting-software market only two years after its introduction.[35]

Five Little Lightbulbs

As complex as the creativity-innovation continuum can be, more often than not, breakthrough implementable ideas come to us as the proverbial "lightbulb" experience. For example:

- Zalman Silber's nearly $9 million entertainment business, New York Skyride, a company offering simulated helicopter tours of New York, sprang from one simple observation: tourists *must* need something to do. Silber reasoned that there was money to be made from offering indoor entertainment for out-of-towners visiting New York, especially on bad-weather days. Using weather-forecasting tools, state-of-the-art entertainment technology, and clever marketing, Silber invented a new option for tourists.[36]

- When two online financial-services competitors were slugging it out by offering increasingly lucrative prizes for registering online at their respective websites, dollarDEX offered the prospective customers the capability to register for *both* companies' prizes at one time from the dollarDEX site. "By making sure that people who registered at our site still were in the running for both sets of prizes, we probably ended up getting more registrants than both of the freebie-giving stock sites combined," says Richard Lai, dollarDEX founder.[37]

- "We must resist the temptation to think that just because we're Nike, all we have to do is show up," says Tim Joyce, vice president of global sales for Nike, Inc. "One way to guard against complacency is to assume an active role in helping our retailers manage their businesses." Joyce's lightbulb was that Nike would benefit from anticipating retail issues even before its customers did. Consequently, Nike began to plan its customers' assortment of products and even envision what their stores should look like. "Anyone can *sell to* someone. But it takes a different set of skills to be able to *plan for* someone."[38]

- Joshua Silver, an experimental physicist and a professor at Oxford University's New College, has come up with an elegant invention. There are more than one billion people in the world who need help with their vision but who don't have access to an eye-care professional. Silver created self-adjusting eyeglasses for which users don't need an optometrist or a prescription. Silver's glasses contain a fluid-filled cell bound by a thin elastic membrane. Turning a knob changes the pressure of the fluid and thus the power of the lenses—a procedure not unlike focusing a pair of binoculars. Silver and some colleagues distributed copies of his invention in a Ghanaian village where no one had eyeglasses. The results were encouraging. "There was a tailor who couldn't work anymore, because he couldn't see close-up," Silver says. "We gave him a pair of these glasses, and he started working again."[39]

- Adi Lipman, a high school student in Tel Aviv, was taking a final exam in English, his second language. "I didn't have a dictionary with me," he says, "so I thought, 'What if there were a device like a pen that I could roll over a word, and it would translate that word for me?'" A talented programmer, he was already working in his father's company, Lipman Engineering, when he had his idea for a translator. He proposed it to his father, and thus the Quicktionary was born—along with a new company, WizCom Technologies Ltd. The Quicktionary uses OCR (optical character recognition) technology that scans a word, goes into a language database, and displays a translation onscreen—all within about three seconds. Quicktionary models are now available in seventeen languages, including English, Hebrew, Korean, and Portuguese.[40]

TrendSmart Tip: Pay attention to innovations in a broad cross-section of industries and companies; they may spur your own company's innovative products and services, which could be your next breakthrough to success!

Traveler's Aids

Some industries are especially prolific when it comes to creative ideas turned into new services. "Innovation is crucial as competition heats up in the hotel market," says KPMG hotel consultant Clay Dickinson. "Learning about guests to anticipate their needs is an important way to keep them coming back," he says. For example:

- Guests staying at the sixty-one-room Fifteen Beacon in Boston get ten business cards with the hotel's address and direct room telephone and fax numbers. Every room has three telephones, including one cellular phone. For the business traveler staying for several days, the benefits of local contact information, and the technological tools provided, are invaluable innovations.
- At the Ritz-Carlton hotel in Atlanta, guests having trouble with their laptops can call a "technology butler" twenty-four hours a day who will come to your room and work on your computer.
- Another hotel has introduced a "butler's closet," a small chamber where the staff places guests' food, and guests can access it when they wish.
- The Bryant Park boutique hotel in New York has a seventy-seat movie theater in its basement. The opportunity to see a first-run movie adds to the overall experience at the hotel.[41]

"The Place of Most Potential"

My friend Dewitt Jones, a *National Geographic* photographer, helps us to understand the nature of creativity. He has made a wonderful video called *Everyday Creativity*, in which Dewitt shows viewers the process he uses to capture the exact image he is looking for. Since the average

Geographic photo assignment uses four hundred rolls of film—more than fourteen thousand shots—to get approximately thirty images, Dewitt makes several key points for all *TrendSmart* leaders about what it takes to deviate from the norm and succeed. Consider these:

- *Find the extraordinary in the ordinary.* Look for something unique. Look at the ordinary, see the extraordinary.
- *There is more than one "right answer."* Assume you can make mistakes, and take chances. Thirty out of fourteen thousand gives you plenty of opportunities.
- *Choose the right perspective, the right "lens."* Sometimes it is better to move in closer to the issue or problem, at other times it is best to stand back. Try all the options until something comes through.
- *Put yourself in the place of most potential.* Trust your sense of where the action is going to be. Know how your tools work and know them so well that you need not have to think about the technical side. Then, when the perfect opportunity comes along, you are ready to seize it.[42]

TrendSmart Tip: Foster and enhance creativity by looking for the extraordinary in the ordinary, looking for more than one "right answer," and regarding a problem from a different perspective.

Creative companies put themselves in the place of most potential to create markets that didn't exist before (Amazon.com). They make the extraordinary out of the ordinary (Starbucks). They choose the right perspective and focus on individual market segments in order to deliver a combination of features that customers in those segments couldn't find elsewhere (Lands' End). They know there is more than one right answer (Dell Computer).

TrendSmart Tips

- Make deviating from the norm the standard, the expected. Think of this as a new kind of "standard deviation."
- Pay attention to innovations in a broad cross-section of industries and companies; they may spur your own company's innovative products and services, which could be your next breakthrough to success!
- Foster and enhance creativity by looking for the extraordinary in the ordinary, looking for more than one "right answer," and regarding a problem from a different perspective.

Chapter 8

Proactive Luck
Where Finding Good Luck Is Not an Entitlement Program

⊕ ⊕ ⊕

"I think we have to believe everything that's reasonable to us."
—Michael McClure, poet

TrendSmart young managers and seasoned leaders alike understand that good luck comes to those who seek it; luck does not just "happen." You become successful these days if you do not leave your luck to chance. You know too that there are ways to leverage your luck, to enhance your chances, and to literally push your luck forward. It takes courage, ingenuity, and creativity.

**TrendSmart Tip: Good luck comes to those
who seek it; luck doesn't just "happen."**

In my last book, *TILT!: Irreverent Lessons for Leading Innovation in the New Economy*, I offered up a term for proactive luck-seeking:

I call it "good lucky," and it is best understood via this story I often tell.

TrendSmart Tip: Leveraging luck takes courage,
ingenuity, and creativity.

"GOOD LUCKY!"

Ever since I was a child, I have looked forward to occasional visits to Chinese restaurants. Even now, as an adult who far too often orders Chinese takeout, the excitement builds as the meal progresses to its culmination: the reading of the fortune cookie!

I admit that I have consumed large quantities of won tons, spring rolls, chow mein, and pot stickers with great alacrity, but when I place that small, bent, brittle cookie in my hand, time stands still. With a mixture of anticipation and trepidation, I slowly place it between my fingers and then, like the quick, painful act of removing a Band-Aid, I snap it and gaze at my future as it struggles to emerge from one half of the cookie.

I hasten to add that it is not just the proposed future that interests me, but, as a writer and poet, the inevitable erroneous translations from Chinese to English are often a treat unto themselves: "You will emerse [*sic*] victorious in all you do." "You will meet someone soon who will change your wife." You get the idea.

So, recently, I was preparing a keynote speech for a global symposium of Sun Microsystems's "SunService" technicians. While sitting in a Chinese restaurant near Sun's Northern California headquarters in the Silicon Valley, I was jotting down my most profound thoughts...on a paper napkin. My role in the symposium was to prod and motivate SunService people to look at the emerging world differently, think "outside the box," be more innovative and unconventional, and thus provide better service.

As I finished my meal, I had roughed out the key points of my talk and had a dozen more ideas rattling in my head. Then I grabbed the cookie. Breaking it open in one quick movement, I shattered the cookie, and the message spun downward in the air like a poorly designed paper airplane. As I picked it up off the floor and read it, I realized that I had in my hand the title for my speech—and a new concept that I had never considered before. The fortune read:

"In love and business you always find good lucky."

Good lucky? Good lucky…in love? Good lucky…in business? What a concept, and what a gift had been given to me. I had not previously considered the role that luck plays in my life and in the lives of successful clients and colleagues. More important, I had not known it was possible to "find" good luck. I had always assumed that on a few special occasions, luck found me.

"Good Lucky" on the High Seas

Just behind any semblance of "luck" is a series of proactive steps long since taken. I clearly recall how I got the best salaried job I ever had prior to my embarking upon the entrepreneurial life. Fresh out of graduate school, and ABD (all but dissertation), I was totally burned out from pushing straight through to get my B.A., my M.A., and my Ph.D. In my mid-twenties then, with only the dissertation left to write, I became restless and started looking for ways to get a salaried job, pay off my loans, and travel…hopefully all at the same time!

I began putting the word out to friends and relatives that I was looking for the next phase to begin, trying to leverage my good-lucky opportunities. I was accepted into the Peace Corps and was slated to go to Africa when someone told me about Semester at Sea, an accredited college program taught on an ocean liner that travels around the world, a semester at a time. Bingo! This was the perfect opportunity for me. But there was one problem: the competition to get hired was monumental. Older, well-traveled, tenured professorial types had the proverbial inside track. What chance did a twenty-four-year-old, unpublished ABD have—one who had only flown on a plane once, from Los Angeles to San Francisco?

Undaunted, I wrote for information and a faculty application form. After leaving blank the lines that asked for books published and years tenured, I completed the form as best I could. Then, I took one last step.

Figuring that my only hope was to find a competitive advantage, I did what any good young entrepreneur in search of some good lucky would do: I found an angle. Taking a bright red felt pen in hand, I scrawled across the application in big, all-cap letters: "I CAN LEAVE WITH 24 HOURS' NOTICE!" Total mobility was my lone competitive advantage.

Sure enough, as good lucky would have it, an older professor took quite ill not long before the ship was to leave for the Semester at Sea. Someone vaguely remembered my application. I got a call on a Friday and had until Monday to accept the job. I jumped at the chance, worked really hard once aboard ship, was voted the most popular teacher, and was asked back twice more. It was the best salaried job I ever had. I got to see the world, got paid for it, and even nibbled away at my student loans. *Very* good lucky, indeed!

Leverage Your Reputation

Ron Kaufman tells a story of advice he recently gave to a gathering of police officers that illustrates another instance of leveraging luck. A police officer asked him, "There are only three thousand of us and three million members of the public. What difference can we really make to improve the quality of service in this country?"

"You have the leverage," Ron replied. "Use it."

Kaufman gives an example of how one officer can have a lasting effect on public perception of his job. Imagine a uniformed police officer making his normal rounds, stopping in front of a busy outdoor café to pick up an empty coffee cup and take it to the trash. "Wouldn't you notice what he had done?" asks Kaufman. "Would you notice his effort, appreciate that small action, and feel good about what he just did to make your city just a little cleaner?"

Small, simple acts can reap disproportionately large rewards, and act you must. These days, good lucky does *not* come to those who wait. Rather, you have to get out there and market, mingle, and schmooze with aplomb and a modicum of chutzpah! As any entrepreneur will tell you, creating opportunities for good lucky requires constant attention.

Good lucky can also be the by-product of good manners and common courtesy. Simple professional acts can enhance your opportunities for good lucky. For example, consider these two scenarios. In scenario one, a job applicant seeks a position that he knows is a long shot. He is told when he applies that only those asked for a second interview will be contacted. He waits several days and hears nothing. In scenario two, he applies for a similar job with another company. Within twenty-four hours, he gets a call thanking him for applying but telling him the position has been filled. Which company is planting future seeds for good lucky? The good lucky is the company that took his application seriously. Down the road, they may benefit from the good experience the applicant had. These days, one disgruntled job seeker—or customer—can influence literally thousands of people's opinions of a company.

Strong organizations should extend good service to everyone—even those they choose not to hire. After all, job applicants have shown an interest in you. Shouldn't you express appreciation back to them? And just imagine if you treated customers with the same disdain every time they browsed in your store and bought nothing.

Finding Talent

Let's assume now that applicants are not flocking to you, but rather you have to find them and interest them in your company. How might using good lucky apply in this situation?

"If you want to hire the next [superstar], you have to recruit that person differently, evaluate him or her differently, and offer him or her a job differently. Looking for a job in the old way can be a horrible, demeaning process," says Professor John Sullivan, head of the human-resource management program at San Francisco State University. He offers a number of examples to illustrate what he means:

- Train your managers to capture the names and coordinates of impressive people they meet at conferences. Over time, you'll develop a talent database.
- Don't just *check* the references that talented applicants provide. Consider the references as job candidates in their own right, and capture their names as well.
- Be sure to ask new hires what people they would recruit from their former company. Why? Because great people tend to know other great people.
- Stay in touch with talented people who leave, and use them as a source of talent leads.[43]

The "Lame Service Awards"

In *TILT!,* I wrote about the "ABCD" awards for service offered "Above and Beyond the Call of Duty." Now it is time for me to create the LSAs—Lame Service Awards—which go out to all those who miss the opportunity for good lucky by doing as little as possible as often as possible.

Unfortunately, the candidate list for LSAs is nearly infinite. For example, a waitress at an Italian restaurant got an LSA when she brought me a teaspoon to twirl my spaghetti. When I asked for a tablespoon, she told me she always uses a teaspoon, that "it works just fine," and turned and left. Another LSA went to a hotel clerk. I had arrived after 6 P.M. due to a late flight, and secured the late arrival with my credit card. While signing in, I overheard the man next to me getting a AAA discount on his room rate. "Oh," I said to the clerk, "I have AAA too." He told me my reservation was not for the AAA rate, nor would he accept a change in my original registration arrangements. I thanked him politely, told him I would gladly give him an LSA for his AAA attitude, and walked across the street to a competing hotel.

Rob Peter *and* Paul

Many times, good lucky is the result of bold, creative, and even risky acts. Consider Steve Healis's atypical after-hours research for Avalon Building Maintenance. Almost nightly, he and his partner donned scruffy clothes, hopped into a van, and drove around Orange County, California, raiding their competitors' dumpsters, in which Healis insists they found "very useful information among the coffee-stained scraps and crumpled Post-its." Healis, who says he and his partner broke no laws digging through the trash, admits they would feign insanity or homelessness if a night watchman happened to spot them.[44]

Doing things unconventionally often brings you closer to good lucky, sooner. Consider these bold actions:

- Rob Ryan, creator of Entrepreneur America, a business boot camp for new entrepreneurs, advises attendees on how to make money. He uses some interesting logic in this metaphor: "One of my basic rules is that you don't rob delicatessens. You rob banks. You have to go where the money is."[45]

- Randy Lagman, technology adventurer outfitter for Lands' End, speaks of polar explorer Will Steger. Lagman equips world-class adventurers like Steger with digital tools for transmitting gripping diaries and stunning photos to the Internet to draw customers to the Lands' End website. But Steger had a new twist to leverage his lucky; he was dropped off at the North Pole by a Russian icebreaker, and his intention was to walk *back*. "That's a different perspective on life from what I'm used to," says Lagman.[46] Planning your route in reverse, as you can see, can get you the attention of corporate sponsors and bring you, therefore, a bit of good lucky.

- After more than thirty international rock-climbing titles, Lynn Hill left competition and joined the elite North Face Extreme Team, continuing to set precedents high in Australia, Sardinia, and Italy's Dolomites. "I don't like the word *impossible*," she muses. "I really hesitate to use that word. *Improbable* works for me, but *impossible* I don't agree with."[47] If you believe that nothing is impossible, only improbable, you greatly increase your chances of finding good lucky.

- You also enhance good lucky when you instill confidence. Actress Renée Zellweger tells a story about her father: "My father put me on the diving board and said, 'Do a somersault.' He never put it in my mind that it was daunting. When you introduce something new without introducing the risk factor at the same time, you instill confidence."[48]

• Good lucky can change your life in an evening. Bill Wear learned how to hack into phone lines when he was ten years old. By age fourteen, he'd become a full-blown computer delinquent. One night, using a password he'd stolen from a guidance counselor, he hacked into his school's computer. But what happened next changed his life. The school counselor, who knew that Wear had swiped the password, had posted a message for him. Wear still recalls it: "I know that you're using my account. I also know about your father. I know he abuses you. I also know that we can do something. Call me. Let me help."[49]

Having been offered some good lucky, Wear made the call. His counselor helped get him into a private school— and stayed in touch with Wear as he earned two engineering degrees. A wise mentor had transformed the life of a hacker. Today the ex-hacker is himself a mentor. He describes his encounter with the counselor in an online handbook for Hewlett-Packard employees who participate in the company's email-mentoring program.

The idealab! Fakeout

idealab! of Pasadena, California, launched by Bill Gross, "seeks to quantify the rules of e-commerce so precisely that lucrative start-ups can be grown like hothouse tomatoes," says Charles Platt. Here, perhaps, lies Gross's secret ingredient for bringing good lucky his way: he bolsters conventional market research by proto-typing each idea as if it were an actual business—for a day, or even a few hours. Sometimes he'll set up a site that appears to be stocked with inventory, although it actually has none. Suppose he sets up a music site and wants to get an idea of volume and viability. He accepts orders via credit cards, though there's no merchant account. "We just throw away the credit card numbers," he says. "We don't charge the customers. We'll go to Tower Records, buy the CDs that people ordered, and send them for free."

His "fakeouts," as he calls them, are quicker and cheaper than running focus groups, and the data is more reliable. By prototyping the business, Gross knows for sure whether consumers will buy the product, because they already think they did! And he can vary parameters to find what works best. "For $5,000 you can check twenty different proposi tions and have absolute hard data on whether people come, how often they come, whether they buy, and what the average order size is."[50]

TrendSmart Tip: Test innovative ideas on a small scale.

Two Heads Are Better than One

Another tool in the good-lucky toolbox is collaboration. To leverage your luck, there are times when you can benefit from working collaboratively. Many hands make the work more productive, and collaboration leverages opportunities that can lead directly, and more quickly, to good lucky.

Inc. magazine brought my attention to Ken Craig and Rusty West. The pair met in 1994, when Craig's company, Spenser Communications, installed cabling for West's software business, Market Scan Information Systems, and they've been friends ever since. "We use each other as sounding boards," says West. They exchange ideas and offer each other solutions to problems.[51] In that sense, they function as a mini version of YPO (Young Presidents Organization) or the AMA (American Management Association), both of which for decades have brought company leaders and executives together for mutual exchange of information and advice as part of their larger missions.

TrendSmart Tip: "Lucky" businesspeople are often successful because they know how to collaborate effectively; good teamwork leverages opportunities.

Drucker's Seven Sources of Opportunity

For some of us, opportunity knocks. For most of us, opportunity slinks under the door in the dead of night. Good lucky often requires skills, tactics, and acts that mirror those of a classic entrepreneur. Highly respected management thinker Peter Drucker has some insights worth examining.

"The entrepreneur's job," says Drucker, "is to pursue systematic, purposeful innovation." The first steps? Keep it simple. Start small. Stay focused. Monitor the trends and indicators that help you spot the opportunities for new business creation:

1. *Look for the unexpected.* Keep your eye out for the forgotten product that suddenly catches on, the service you're not focusing on but that customers seem to want, or an unexpected trend, such as the surprising rise in the number of books bought by Americans year after year—a trend that has spawned huge chains of bookstores.

2. *Watch for incongruities.* A discrepancy between what is and what ought to be—indicated, for example, by widespread dissatisfaction—may offer you an opportunity. A case in point: OM Scott was once just another struggling lawn-products company, and customers applied its products every which way, with uneven results. Then Scott invented its big hit, the Spreader, which finally allowed customers to apply the products in the right proportions.

3. *Fill a process need.* Finding the missing link or bottleneck

in some sort of process can bring good lucky. Eye surgeons long knew how to do cataract surgery. An enzyme that made the process easier had been known for decades but wasn't usable because it was too hard to preserve. In the 1950s, an entrepreneur named William Connor figured out how to preserve the enzyme, thereby closing the circle.

4. *Understand industry and market structures.* Think outsourcing. Think deregulation, as in trucking or telecommunications or energy. When some big event or trend changes the way an industry does business, entrepreneurs can usually figure out how to elbow their way in.

5. *Know thy demographics.* Shifts in the population, both in space and in time, nearly always open up business niches.

6. *Note changes in perception.* Americans, for example, are healthier and living longer, yet they're more worried than ever about getting sick and growing old. The result is a booming market in health care and nutritional products and advice.

7. *Find new knowledge first.* "Drucker puts this source last on the list because it's the chanciest—in part because new inventions...usually attract dozens of competitors," observes John Case. "There's an explosion of entrepreneurship, then a shakeout that destroys most of the startups." Drucker writes, "After that period is over, entry into the industry is foreclosed for all practical purposes."[52]

So, as we have seen, good lucky is part science, part art, part hard work, and part chutzpah! A crucial step in this process, as Drucker has reminded us, is having good information and trends in your grasp. These trends can then guide your decision making and strategy.

TrendSmart **Tips**

- Good luck comes to those who seek it; luck doesn't just "happen."
- Leveraging luck takes courage, ingenuity, and creativity.
- Test innovative ideas on a small scale.
- "Lucky" businesspeople are often successful because they know how to collaborate effectively; good teamwork leverages opportunities.

PART TWO

The TrendSmart Consumer

Overview:

Know Thy Customer

Having a clear and current understanding of emerging trends for companies and organizations is a crucial element of the mindset of today's *TrendSmart* leaders. Part of the power of this book comes from a thorough grasp of two other key factors: knowing thy customer and knowing thy employees.

In part 2, we will explore six new and evolving trends that affect consumer behavior, values, and buying preferences. As with all trends in this book, the exponential advantage will go to those *TrendSmart* leaders who can develop strategies that address several trends concurrently, given the needs and goals of their companies at a given point in time. As you read the trends in part 2, therefore, be mindful of those in part 1, for it is in the integration of trend data that the whole truly becomes greater than the sum of its parts.

Chapter 9

Mass Customization

Where One Size No Longer Fits All...One Size Fits One

⊕ ⊕ ⊕

"If the poem is made right, it will sit well in any room."

—*Lew Welsh, poet*

Michael Dell, founder of Dell Computers, first popularized the term "mass customization" many years ago. Dell understood—at a very young age, and far sooner than his then-megacorporate competitors—that the values, habits, and needs of the consumer were changing at least as fast as the speed of technology. What Moore's Law was to the very essence of exponential technological change, Dell's Law was to the rate of change among consumers. People wanted choices. People wanted quality. People wanted trustworthy brands. People wanted exactly the computer for their needs. And people wanted *all* of this—*fast!* What he understood, and what every manager needs still to understand, is that one size no longer fits all; rather, there is in consumers' psyches the idea that they are indeed the center of the universe—that one size fits only one.

Like a good trend analyst, Michael Dell connected the pixels and made a very profitable picture from them.

TrendSmart Tip: For successful customer service today, keep in mind that "one size fits only one": the customer you're serving *right now*. Mass customization means you need to treat each customer individually.

How "The Surf Doctor" Treats His Patients

Even in the health-care and professional-services industries, the need for mass customization often is the differentiator in the marketplace. A physician, for example, may have set protocols for diagnosis and treatment, and yet can find ways to make the patient feel special. Consider the case of San Francisco's "surf doctor."

Doc Renneker, as his patients affectionately call him, was always a little different. An avid surfer, he took a little longer to get through medical school because every winter, when the waves grew bigger, Doc would leave medical school to follow his passion.

When he set up his own office, his love of surfing was undiminished, and so he instructed his staff to schedule his appointments with patients using a tide book as a guide to his availability.

This is not to imply that he was violating his Hippocratic oath—quite the contrary. Doc Renneker found that by keeping active in surfing he found the balance and renewed energy to give much more to his patients than most of his colleagues were able to give.

In fact, Doc takes his patients so seriously that he often acts as their champion or ombudsman as they face serious medical decisions with little idea of the available options. Noticing that an increasing number of new patients were coming to him to get second opinions, Doc took out an ad in the *San Francisco Chronicle* for only one day. It said: "Are you at a disadvantage in your dealings with doctors and hospitals? Do you want the most up-to-date information on medical research and treatment? Then contact The Medical Equalizer!"

The response was overwhelming. People with chronic pain contacted him. Even the past president of the California Medical Association began to work with Doc and his patients.

Intuitively knowing what was needed, Doc recently took one of his patients—a thirty-nine-year-old man with bone cancer—for a long walk on a beach. That was their "office visit." Doc then excused himself to go out and catch a few waves while the patient waited on the shore.

"Watching Doc riding those waves," the patient said, "is a perfect metaphor for what Doc's done for me. He's out there to ride the wave as long as he can in the toughest of surf. I guess that's what he wants to do for me too—keep me going as long as possible."

Personalizing for All

Of course, the good doc was putting a human spin on an often-routinized process of health care. This is what mass customization is all about though, finding—and doing—whatever it takes to make the customer feel special.

The rise of mass customization did not occur in a vacuum, as there were structural precursors of it for more than four decades, dating back to the seminal work of W. Edwards Deming. Further, in order to make every product idiosyncratic, breakthroughs in just-in-time manufacturing had to be fairly sophisticated. Tracking of the full order and fulfillment cycle had to be in place. Transaction-management software and accounting was also a given. But even more important, there had to be a shift in *mind-set*, one that took as a "strategic given" that the irrefutable trend was from what I have called "consumer" to "prosumer."

Prosumers are proactive. They want choices and they consciously research their own options. They network with friends, seeking advice and counsel regarding products, but ultimately they believe that *they* are in control of the selection of products and services...and that price is not the independent variable, but quality is. As has been emblazoned on the walls of my favorite Italian restaurant, La Ginestra, in Mill Valley, California, for more than thirty-five years, "Quality Always Wins."

TrendSmart Tip: Turn your consumers into "prosumers," proactive buyers who have a choice of what product or service to buy, and they'll *choose yours* because you've given them the options and the features they truly want.

In Scandinavia, for example, many executives have gone so far as to customize the quality of access to them. Whereas in America high-ranking executives print their general office number on their business card, in Finland, even presidents of large corporations print their personal mobile-phone numbers on their cards. "Here, people think mobile phones give them power because of who can call them," comments Helsinki Telephone's Risto Linturi.[53]

Get Involved in Your Customers' Lives

My friend Chip Conley is in the hospitality business. As the founder and owner of Joie d' Vivre hotels, which manages nearly twenty properties, one would think that Chip could sit back and watch the revenue flow. Not so.

Since all of his hotels are small boutique venues catering to a targeted prosumer, Chip is very "hands on."[54] For example, at his Phoenix Hotel, which caters to artists and performers visiting San Francisco, he once baby-sat Sinead O'Connor's new baby when she had to do a show at Slim's (and observed that mother and child "were both bald"). He made it a point to introduce performance artist Karen Finley and photographer Andre Serrano (of "Piss Christ" fame), both National Endowment for the Arts winners, when they happened to be staying at the Phoenix at the same time. He brought film director Wim Wenders and Laurie Anderson together in the Phoenix courtyard. He fended off groupies hungry for a touch of the late rock star Kurt Cobain.

Ask Your Clients What They Want

In researching this book, I came upon one of the finest examples of an organization doing many things the "right" ways; that is, in ways that foreshadow emerging ironic trends: Griffin Hospital of Derby, Connecticut.

For starters, when trying to better understand the specific needs of its prosumer patients, Griffin took the radical step of asking its patients what they wanted! Further, after finding out what they wanted, Griffin did a really odd thing: it gave them *all* of it. In doing so, Griffin radically reformed its culture in a change-allergic industry.[55] Let's look at more of the specifics.

The music in the parking lot? The double beds? The magic act in the patient lounge? The banana muffins baking in one of the cozy kitchens found on every wing of every floor? Patients wanted it and patients got it.

What Griffin's homegrown, do-it-yourself makeover suggests is that it is uncompromising behavior that makes real change possible. It also makes mass customization more than a business buzzword.

At Griffin, which serves a mix of the modestly white-collar and the working-class ethnic groups in south central Connecticut, patient satisfaction has soared to 96 percent—an astounding level in any industry; one that's almost unheard of in the hospital business.

TrendSmart Tip: Get to know the *specific needs* of your customers—and then develop products and services that meet those needs.

Griffin's secret? A clear, three-step recipe that any organization can follow to similar success:

- First, cultivate an obsession with reconceptualizing every element of the business around customers' desires.
- Second, implement the resulting insights with the sort of thoroughness and attention to detail usually reserved for, say, manned space flight.
- And finally, be really, really nice. All the time. To everyone.

For example, Griffin passed out detailed questionnaires to its obstetrics patients, as well as to new and expectant mothers who had chosen to use other hospitals, and ran focus groups. After a few months, the executives had assembled an impressive maternity wish list, which they readily granted. Specifically, not only did mothers want their husbands present during delivery, but many wanted their children and their own parents in the birthing room, too. They wanted rooms that didn't look like hospital rooms. They wanted double beds, so their husbands or whoever could sleep next to them. They wanted Jacuzzis. They wanted big windows and skylights. They wanted fresh flowers. They wanted big, comfortable lounges where the family could gather. They wanted nurses who paid close attention to them and doctors who followed up on problems.

Hospital admitting processes are often intimidating at best and focused on insurance companies at worst. Not at Griffin. Once you've registered, someone leads you to the appropriate wing—it's not good enough to merely give you directions. Pointing is actually banned in hallways. "Being taken to your unit by a person is something you remember," says Bill Powanda, vice president of support services at Griffin.

Praise also goes to Griffin's large health-resource center, open to the public, which has medical books aimed at laypeople and computers linked to health-related websites.

Perhaps best of all, patients point out that they are constantly being bombarded by "unexpected acts of kindness." Now, compare Griffin Hospital with your own. Which would you prefer?

Very quietly, the trend toward prosumption has been met by new customer-service attitudes as well. *TrendSmart* leaders' customer-service mind-sets are focused on the "one" among the "many." These leaders make each customer feel unique, yet they also know how very many customers it will take to grow the bottom line. Obviously, the days of one-dimensional sales and marketing strategies are gone forever.

Customer Service the French Way

My administrative assistant, Ann Luckiesh, recently shared with me an extraordinary example of making the customer feel very, very special. While her daughter, Erin, was traveling aboard France's TGV train during a summer college excursion, a number of delays ensued that caused all passengers to arrive quite late. Nearly two months later, Erin, now back in California, received the following letter from the rail-system executive. For your convenience, I have had the letter translated.

Exhibit 9-1: How One Company Apologized for Its Extreme Customer-Service Delays

On June 25, 2001, the TGV aboard which you were traveling encountered grave difficulties caused by a series of incidents that heavily affected the traffic of TGV Mediterranee.

You arrived at your destination with significant delay, which most certainly aggravated you.

I insist on personally apologizing on behalf of the SNCF for all the difficulties you may have encountered during your trip.

To make up for all troubles that affected your trip, I have decided to fully compensate you for the price of your ticket in the form of a Bon Voyage bonus.

I would also like to give you the reasons for the unusual delay you have experienced.

Close to Marseille, the spontaneous fire of several cables affected our traffic lights and railings and required safety measures such as stopping and then reducing the speed of the TGV.

Later, the rails were mobilized by the equipment necessary to verify the state of things. Traffic could only be started again when verification was completed. Finally, near the station of Valence TGV, a TGV was damaged by an animal running into it and was forced to slow down, which also delayed the following trains.

The accumulations of all trains slowing down as well as the ones that were stopped completely disorganized our TGV Mediterranee's traffic.

I know you've encountered a painful moment, and once again, on behalf of the SNCF, I apologize and hope that in spite of the circumstances, you will travel with us again.

This "Bon Voyage coupon" is accepted for its value in payment for all travels offered by SNCF (except within Paris) at all train stations and travel agencies. Good until July 17, 2002.

This is mass customization above and beyond the call of duty. The Bon Voyage coupon was worth nearly $50 U.S. The value in terms of future travel on TGV? Priceless.

**TrendSmart Tip: Go above and beyond the call of duty.
If you've made a mistake and delivered poor customer
service, apologize and make up for it. Your customers
will love you and will continue to be good customers.**

Mass Food for Thought

We have seen how industries as diverse as health care and hotels have
met the needs of the prosumer. We turn now to some other examples
of American industries whose overt focus is on customer satisfaction:
retailers, grocers, and food-service providers. These industries have
been especially committed to supporting the technology and training
that are required to succeed at mass customization.

The Gap, for example, noticed that its customer base was, as an
aggregate, shifting in tastes and purchasing patterns. It also took note
of emerging competition, the enormous power of branding, and the
internal need to grow shareholder value. The resultant initiative? Old
Navy.

Several major grocers and other vendors have stayed closely in
touch with their customers, too. As the pace of life has sped up, time
itself has become a commodity. Recognizing this, it is no accident
that one of the fastest-growing grocery sections contains prepackaged
fresh salad "kits." Open bag. Poor into bowl. Bingo! Your salad is
ready.

No industry has been in closer touch with the prosumer than the
restaurant business. Many midscale chains, such as Outback Steak-
house and Chevy's, have very sophisticated point-of-sale information,
region by region, restaurant by restaurant, server by server, and guest
by guest.

In America, even the national pastime, baseball, has seen major
changes spearheaded in part by a better understanding of what fans

want. The tremendous number of new ballparks, incorporated into the centers of communities, with ease of access and lots of options for food and fun, are almost metaphors for the importance of mass customization for sustainable success today.

Is Online Off Base for Customers?

Technology, too, can be an agent of mass customization for the prosumer. Few advances have gotten more press and hype than the Internet. But, cautions Christopher Selland, vice president of The Yankee Group's e-Business Strategies Research and Consulting Group, the Internet is a tool. Like any tool, it has an identifiable preferred use.

"Remember, the Internet was not built for commerce and it was not built for selling—it was built for research. And this is how your customers, my customers, and everybody's customers are using it," says Selland. "The role of technology is not to empower the sale, it is to empower the customer."[56]

Anna Muoio has identified several websites with features that the savvy prosumer likes.[57]

Exhibit 9-2: Websites with Features That Prosumers Like

- The Nine West Online Store (www.ninewest.com) includes a "your shopping bag" feature that keeps a running tally of your purchases. There is no need to do your own math, and are no surprises at checkout time.
- The Lands' End site (www.landsend.com) features a service that lets you order free fabric swatches. They arrive by mail, so you can actually see and feel them.

- Email response from Cosmetics Counter (www. cosmeticscounter.com) directs the customer to interact with, yes, a live person! Fragrance Counter (www.fragrancecounter.com) works the same way.
- Garden.com (www.garden.com) offers a one-year, 110 percent satisfaction guarantee that is unrivaled in the world of e-commerce.
- Amazon.com (www.amazon.com) posts a customer's Bill of Rights that is fair, honest, and to the point.
- Gap Online (www.gap.com) has a section called "gap-style," which uses photographs of actual clothes to help you put together your own outfit. As you add items to your outfit, the site keeps a running tally of your purchases.
- Buying jeans at Levi.com (www.levi.com) is actually fun.

A Customer's "Mess" May Be Your Opportunity

Even with advanced technology, in many arenas there is no substitute for face-to-face service, which no website could ever provide.

For example, a dad comes into a restaurant for lunch with his six-year-old son. Halfway through the meal, the child fidgets and knocks his drink on the floor. The restaurant now has what a Taco Bell executive once described to me as "OBM"—one big mess! What should the restaurant staff do?

First, take charge of the situation. Take care of the dad. He may be embarrassed or worried about buying another drink. So, replace the drink with a bigger drink and an even bigger smile. Second, put the child at ease. In his mind, there may be some real concern about his dad's possible reaction, as well as the staring eyes of other customers. So reassure him too. Third, clean up the mess quickly and unobtrusively. Fourth, bring along a side order of fries or a nice piece of pie...something extra, unexpected; something that will be remembered long after the spill is forgotten. Do not worry about all your customers beginning to tip over their drinks willy nilly. If other customers have been watching from the beginning, and everyone does, they'll be as relieved—and impressed—as the father and son.

When you are already in the lead, to stay far ahead of your competition you need to seek out *new* ways to differentiate yourself, new ways to surprise and delight your customers. Turn a mess into a message, and in so doing, you will acquire a good customer. When your customers win, you win.

A Bonus: Customizing Customers and Employees

Mass customization has been generally understood in the context of customer satisfaction. But for some time now I have proposed that many of the principles of customer relationship management (CRM) and mass customization apply equally well to employee productivity and retention. Understanding this can make or break a company, since many studies report that losing a single key employee can cost a company more than $100,000.

Kepner-Tregoe of Princeton, New Jersey, got something of a surprise when it sought to measure turnover costs at fifteen companies. Only five companies could complete the questionnaire. A manufacturer found the loss of a machinist cost $102,796. The termination of an automaker's human-resource manager cost $133,803. The bill accompanying the exit of a fast-food chain store manager tallied $21,931.

But surprise turned to disbelief when adding in "soft" costs, including the loss of intellectual capital, decreased morale, increased employee stress, and negative reputation. The study found the connection between employee loyalty and profits "unassailable."[58]

Mass customization can occur in a large multinational company or at a local "mom and pop" operation. Mass customization exemplifies how the trends that are described in this book interact with one another and help shape strategy and profitability.

TrendSmart Tips

- For successful customer service today, keep in mind that "one size fits only one": the customer you're serving *right now*. Mass customization means you need to treat each customer individually.
- Turn your consumers into "prosumers," proactive buyers who have a choice of what product or service to buy, and they'll *choose yours* because you've given them the options and the features they truly want.
- Get to know the *specific needs* of your customers—and then develop products and services that meet those needs.
- Go above and beyond the call of duty. If you've made a mistake and delivered poor customer service, apologize and make up for it. Your customers will love you and will continue to be good customers.

Chapter 10

Local Universals

Where You Act Locally and Think Globally—and Vice Versa!

⊕ ⊕ ⊕

"It is increasingly evident that solitude is no longer feasible, for the wilderness is no longer man's problem, except how to preserve it."
—*William Everson, poet*

Today, products, services, customers, and employees are all conveniently located just a keyboard or mouse click or cell-phone call away. With so much information instantly available from all over the world, it is now possible for a consumer to research a product at 9 A.M., get the information he needs by 9:05 A.M., and make a purchasing decision by 9:06 A.M. Universal and global input can be applied locally.

The net effect of the Internet, as I often say, is that it has enabled both speed and information to join forces on behalf of the consumer.

As a result, consumers worldwide have become increasingly sophisticated and proactive in their choices of goods and services.

It happens everywhere. A landscaper in Sweden orders gardening supplies online from a company in California. A chef in California buys a special skillet from a company in Sweden. A passenger on a train from London to Surrey buys and sells stocks listed on the Tokyo Exchange via one click of his Palm Pilot. A Toronto woman orders a leather attaché case with her initials on it from France. A Papuan missionary orders communion wafers from Chicago.

Search Globally, Buy Locally

Being a baseball player and a prosumer (see chapter 9), I went online to research the price, quality, features, and return policies of baseball-glove manufacturers. I settled on two gloves, a Wilson A-2000 and a Nakona soft leather twelve-inch fielder's glove. I did comparisons of the two, made mental notes, and determined the pros and cons of each. But before buying either, I called the local store: family-run, forty-year-old T & B Sporting Goods in San Rafael, California. Though their prices were about 15 percent higher, I bought my A-2000 from them because of their return policy: if it needs repair, they'll replace it. They will deal with the manufacturer, the sales rep, and the refunds. I knew they meant it because the prior year, when a new aluminum bat I had purchased started to "buzz," they replaced it with a new one *and* gave me the used one too when it was repaired by the manufacturer. I had searched globally, bought locally.

TrendSmart Tip: Consumers can research products available anywhere in the world, within minutes, using the Internet...but they still want to buy locally. Make sure your company makes it easy for them to do both.

Developing Products for Consumers' Local Tastes

Ron Kaufman is a veritable treasure chest of customer-service stories, some of which help shape this chapter. For example, he tells an insightful story of Italian food, Filipino style, for the Filipino prosumer that illustrates how important it is to develop products for local tastes, even if—especially if—you work for a global company.

"This month I spoke for the store managers and franchisees of Jollibee (hamburgers) and Greenwich (pizza pasta) restaurants in the Philippines. These guys are *really good* at what they do, holding the No. 1 and No. 2 positions in the national quick-service market." (McDonalds runs third, Pizza Hut fourth. These multinationals have *not* been closing the gap!)

Kaufman is a vegetarian, so he didn't taste the hamburgers at Jollibee. But he did try the Greenwich Garden Pizza, and it was quite a memorable experience! The pizza was covered with sweet tomato sauce and the cheese on top was cheddar! In most places, a pizza comes with a tangy tomato sauce and mozzarella cheese, right? So sweet sauce and cheddar? That's no way to make a pizza…unless you want to sell a *lot* of pizzas in the Philippines!

You see, Greenwich doesn't *care* what pizza is known for in Italy or New York, or anywhere else for that matter. Greenwich wants to dominate in the Philippines, and as far as they're concerned, Philippine taste buds rule. Local customers want sweet? Sweet sauce it is. Local customers prefer cheddar? Spread on the cheddar cheese!

**TrendSmart Tip: Develop products for your customers'
local tastes—whether you're making pizzas or
offering sophisticated consulting services.**

I recall a similar experience I had while traveling in Mombassa, Kenya, a city best known for the huge elephant-tusk arches that span the main road into town. At a large restaurant, I ordered "pizza," and what arrived was a slice of white bread, some catsup, and a processed cheese spread partially melted. I could barely eat it, but I could not help but notice many local patrons ordering two or three at a sitting.

Localized mass customization is really quite an amazing revelation. Global brands like Pizza Hut, Shakey's, and Domino's all do business in the Philippines, but their market share is much lower than that of Greenwich. Why? They *know* how to make a great pizza. Their recipe matches the *global* pizza standard. Yet prosumers in the Philippines and Kenya wouldn't touch it.

Prosumer preferences for mass customization touch many aspects of business today. In addition to just-in-time manufacturing and inventory, recent advances in detailed "data mining" of a specific customer's preferences have enhanced the ability of countless companies to design, build, and deliver customized products while remaining highly profitable. No detail is too small, and every detail can enhance the customer's experience. In this sense, we are all in the pizza business.

Gaining a Competitive "Advanex"

One of the ironic trends *TrendSmart* leaders understand is that today, even in a global economy, there are advantages to thinking locally and acting locally. For example, Advanex is a global organization whose head office is in Japan. They make springs ranging from microscopic to monstrous. More of note here, Advanex articulates unique mission statements for each company and department in its global network. In this way, everyone realizes that they are part of a bigger team and a bigger purpose while having a localized version of their mission that makes sense in each disparate location.

The Advanex Corporate Office Mission is unique: "To provide 'Eureka!'" In describing Advanex, author Ron Kaufman asks, "How many corporate offices do you know that promise such excitement?"

Paul Kato, grandson of the founder, insists upon "glocalization"—global concepts adapted in language to impact the local population. In this way, mission statements match the local market and culture. Here are some examples of "glocalized" Advanex mission statements that Kaufman identified:

- *For Singapore:* "It's value time!" Singaporeans are passionate about gaining value and saving time.
- *For Malaysia:* "World class team, world class results." Malaysians are always keen to achieve "world class" status.
- *For Hong Kong:* "Making tomorrow happen today." Hong Kong is a key to China's future, but it is committed to real profits right now.
- *For England:* "Shaping the future with pride." From the country that created Rolls-Royce, what other articulation would suffice?
- *For California:* "Create opportunities, increase satisfaction." This one was created for a team of recent immigrants to the United States.
- *For Japan:* "365247." The company promises instant availability and immediate, non-stop response. Get the message?

"Every culture gets turned on by unique goals and aspirations," says Kaufman. This is true of national and ethnic groups as well as occupations. Who crafted the mission of your department or organization? Is it relevant and inspiring? Does it focus your people toward goals they desire, and motivate them to achieve? "If so," he adds, "you will certainly grow. If not, you're not so hot."

KPG Crafts a Powerful Intention

Kaufman also alerts us that the Singapore-based business world of Kodak Polychrome Graphics (KPG) is always changing. This provider of hard-copy reproductions makes a promise to customers that's clear and focused. It helps them stay on track.

Their promise is:

- To be a company that changes technology. Not just a company that changes with it.
- To be where our customers are. Here and around the world.
- To be a company that focuses on one industry. Our customers' industry.
- To anticipate our customers' needs. And exceed them.
- To be a partner. Not just a vendor.
- Last, but far from least, to be a company that keeps its promises.

Ambitious? Perhaps. Far-fetched? Hardly. Promises are made to be kept. You can, as Kaufman points out, shape the culture in your company, department, or organization. Start with a powerful intention; know where you want to go, then be deliberate with your directions. Select words and images to inspire your team, support it all with consistent actions undertaken with clarity and passion, and watch your culture blossom.

Work Globally, Live Locally

This global consumer behavior is mirrored by shifts in employment options, as workers move easily and interchangeably from global to local and back many times daily. Ironically, as global commerce expands, it is increasingly easy to stay closer to home. For example, a woman in the Philippines does data entry for her employer in Iowa. Her paycheck is electronically wired to her local bank. Her ATM card allows her to buy bottled water from France, which she drinks while doing data entry...and so on...and so on. In this sense then, we are all becoming "stationary immigrants," moving around the world from our desks, our minds wandering like itinerant vagabonds. The world, indeed, is now conveniently located in the crags and crevices of our own cerebral cortex.

Techy-Feely

The ability to move around the world without leaving our desks is both liberating and isolating. Consequently, the much-chronicled relationship of high-tech and high-touch has never been more prevalent. With every advance of technology has come a commensurate increase in the need for friends, family, and the human element. There has been a dramatic increase, for example, in the sale of hand-held organizers as well as in the sale of movie tickets. I have often pointed out that the rise of Starbucks in the United States almost exactly parallels the rise in technology-driven products and jobs.

The leadership of Starbucks seems to understand the dehumanizing side of high-tech and that people would increasingly want more human contact, however brief—or caffeinated!

Maverick entrepreneur Anita Roddick, founder of The Body Shop, accurately observes, "There is an incredible sense of isolation in the world today. Any young person who finds an antidote to loneliness will have found a business that will last forever."[59] Consequently, it is to a company's advantage to provide workers with more than a job, but also with a sense of meaning.

High-tech/high-touch lives on in the form of what my research editor, Laurie Masters, calls "techy-feely."

Polishing Stones

Today's managers engage in local *and* global actions simultaneously, possessing the ability to gather enormous amounts of information on the most obscure topics readily. In many instances, the ability to think locally *or* globally to find the right answers to the right questions will give you a competitive advantage. This deluge of data has served to make it easier to be aware of new ideas and innovations. Increasingly, smart managers and savvy companies are finding their greatest profitability by leveraging the ideas of others.

For example, UK-based Lloyds TSB has been tracking trends in the banking industry for clues and tips for new business endeavors. They watch what competitors are doing worldwide, and they have little concern that a new venture has to be invented by them. In that sense, they are metaphorically in the gemology business, polishing "stones" found elsewhere to make them shine for customers and shareholders.

In my consulting work with Lloyds, I would venture to say that when they have struggled, it has often been because they veered from this strategy. When they are on track, it is in great part because they realize that their forte is implementing rather than generating ideas. "Not invented here" can be a great asset. When companies lose their specificity and focus, they lose business.

TrendSmart Tip: Track your competition around the world to stay on top of local trends.

A World of Change Close to Home

Another aspect of specificity and focus is the growing complexity of international commerce. Multinational companies are now forced to implement their global strategies within the limits of local customs and cultures. These companies increasingly reflect local work styles and labor regulations.

For example, the decision-making process in Finland may differ from that in other countries: "Decisions don't wait to trickle down through the hierarchy, and contacts between companies don't always go through formal channels," explains Risto Linturi, principal research fellow for the Helsinki Telephone Corporation.[60]

When Jeff Davis became president of Via Systems Europe, his CEO, Tim Conlon, presented him with the challenge of rapid revitalization and revamping of several manufacturing plants. In Holland, where labor laws make it very difficult to terminate an employee, he reluctantly agreed to pay nearly $700,000 U.S. to remove a plant manager. That agreement represented nearly twenty times that employee's annual salary.

In a turbo-fast changing world, local flexibility and resiliency are crucial to remaining competitive. Therefore, companies need to understand the opportunities and limitations in the local environment.

TrendSmart Tips

- Consumers can research products available anywhere in the world, within minutes, using the Internet...but they still want to buy locally. Make sure your company makes it easy for them to do both.
- Develop products for your customers' local tastes—whether you're making pizzas or offering sophisticated consulting services.
- Track your competition around the world to stay on top of local trends.

Chapter II

Instant Branding

Where "The Big Idea" Meets the Big Brand

⊕ ⊕ ⊕

"There's nothing more important than having a
good business reputation…[and] you cannot build a
reputation on what you intend to do."

—*Liz Smith*

We turn now to the topic of brands. Brands create customer
expectations of quality and consistency, and in so doing create
a reputation. These days, that reputation may be achieved in a matter of days. Yet, ironically, in the face of blurry-fast change, the key
strengths of a brand become even more important.

Today, we can expect to outlive many of our most popular brands.
Eighteen of the top fifty global brands did not exist twenty years ago.
This is testimony to the pace of brand recognition today.

A good brand is like a good friend; it inspires trust and resonates with our core values. The problem is, today our friendly brands come and go. And, where brands used to be seasoned over time, today they can be bought and sold. In the U.K., Abel Hadden & Company has gone so far as to make "reputation creation" its primary focus. What a zany world we live in.

Two factors dramatically affect the creation and longevity of a brand. First is "the big idea." Second, there is what GMO ad agency cofounder Mike Moser calls a "brand road map." Throughout this chapter, we will examine the big idea and the brand road map in more detail.

TrendSmart Tip: Good organizations need both a richly compelling big idea and a clever, evolving brand road map.

Big Ideas

"Today's marketplace is a war of ideas. Unless you stand for something, you won't stand out," says the U.K.'s Robert Jones in his book, *The Big Idea.*[61] One section of his book strikes me as so important that I want to now allow ample time to highlight some of his key points.

When advertising agencies rave about the "brand experience" or "brand promise," they are clearly talking about something more than a company's product or service—they are referring to a *relationship* with consumers built on emotional ties based in trust, consistent quality, and confidence. From Nike to Starbucks to Coca-Cola, the "sell" is often based upon the bonds that consumers have forged with those brands; what is being sold is far more than tennis shoes, coffee, or colored, carbonated sugar water.

In *The Big Idea,* Jones analyzes fifty of the world's best-known brands and the big ideas behind each of them, and deduces how entrepreneurs can find and communicate their own big ideas. "People don't just *buy* IKEA," says Jones, "they *buy into* it—into an idea that mingles style, thrift, self-help, plainness, Scandinavia, classlessness and all sorts of other things." A brand with emotional content, he says, is always greater than the sum of its parts, and it stands alone.

Jones believes that today's economy recognizes the power of emotion—to challenge complacent corporations, destroy old categories, and bring customers and employees together in completely new kinds of community. "Emotional logic," as Jones calls it, plays a crucial role in today's consumer buying trends. "The things people buy—products and services—are becoming more and more similar as it becomes increasingly easy for one company to copy another's technological advantage," Jones writes. "This has a simple but devastating consequence: in the absence of economic differences, emotional logic will become the single most important business driver."

What's the Big Idea?

Consequently, Jones says that formulating and managing a compelling big idea is the most fundamental of all business objectives. So what are the distinguishing ingredients of a big idea? He cites four key points, each of which is briefly described below. A big idea is:

- *More emotional than a business model.* Business models like these may well generate revenue, but such models are not the kind of big idea that communicates what a business stands for, for its employees and its customers. Business models are, therefore, easy to imitate. The business model targets some way of making money (even if it's in the distant future), but the big idea engages people.

TrendSmart Tip: A business model targets some way of making money, but a big idea engages people...so a good business plan should be coupled with a big idea.

- *More sensuous than ideology.* The last three decades have seen organizations search for corporate identities. Ad-agency executives like Wally Olins preached the value of making your identity visible through consistent use of symbols, logotypes, colors, and typefaces, and the rise of corporate identity coincided with the rise of the diversified corporation.

- *More solid than vision.* Most mission statements not only fail to inspire, but worse still, they are wordy testaments to tunnel vision and lack the ability to capture a big idea. Such formulaic mission statements leave employees under-whelmed. Develop a mission statement that truly inspires and states clearly what you believe.

- *Deeper than brand.* By the end of the century, the idea of brand, in its original form, started to look inadequate. "What organizations started to look for was something deeper than brand," says Jones, "something that, unlike product idea or business model, would be rich and sensu-ous. And something that, unlike vision or brand, would appeal to people inside and outside the organization equally: something they could share."

Bigger—and Better—Ideas

Since often the mission is too internal, and the brand too external, the big idea must come before the brand and the mission. It must drive the kind of promise that the organization makes to its cus-tomers, employees, and shareholders.

"Howard Schultz was once asked by *USA Today* how he created Starbucks as a huge brand," recounts Jones. His response was that "he didn't set out to create a brand; he set out to create a really good company, and the brand developed. In other words, get the big idea right, and its external manifestation, the brand, will to a large extent take care of itself."

"A big idea that can create or nourish a really good company must probably do four things, for both outsiders and insiders," says Jones. "First, it must make the organization valuable. The organization must meet people's real needs—tomorrow's as well as today's, and emotional as well as practical. Second, it must make the organization different— the organization must offer something unique. This is essential if customers are going to buy from it—and if employees are going to work for it. Third, it must bind people together, creating a sense of belonging for employees and customers. Fourth, it must celebrate people's differences. A big idea creates unity but never uniformity."

That's what an organization like Starbucks can do. At Starbucks, people don't just buy coffee, they engage in the whole Starbucks idea of community. Creating depth of engagement means appealing to people at levels other than the purely rational. This intimacy is far more effective for organizations than vision or brand. People become much more than customers or employees; they become participators, creators, and advocates.

TrendSmart Tip: Effective brand-building companies create depth of engagement, which means appealing to customers at levels other than the purely rational...and this intimacy is far more effective for organizations than vision or brand.

Something Old, Something New, Something...Big

What's emerging from all this isn't just big ideas; it's a new kind of corporation. "There's a new way of running a business," says Hans Snook of the U.K.'s Orange mobile phone company. "It's based on integrity, on believing what you say and attempting to deliver on it." Exhibit 11-1 contrasts how old organizations differ from new organizations.

Exhibit 11-1. How Old Organizations Differ from New Organizations

OLD ORGANIZATIONS	NEW ORGANIZATIONS
Customer driven	Stand for something
Seek loyalty	Inspire belief
Use vision and brand as tools	Have big ideas as brand foundation

---

So how is this new way of running a business different? Old organizations claim to be "customer driven." The new organization stands for something. It proposes something that customers then engage in. It doesn't wait for customers to tell it what to do. Big-idea companies gain stature by refusing to pander to customer demands if those demands would undermine the big idea.

Old organizations aimed to win the loyalty of their customers and employees. The new organization goes beyond loyalty. Someone once said, sadly, "Loyalty is what remains when belief has gone." Companies with a big idea inspire belief—something more intelligent, more deeply motivating, more dynamic, something that can make them want to change the way they behave.

Old organizations use vision and brand as tools. New organizations see their big idea not as a tool but as their source of a competitive advantage. They exist to make their big idea a reality and so, in one way or another, "to nourish life."

That's just what we're seeing in the world's marketplace. Amazon, which sells books and other products, is actually about "completeness" and choice. Consider these others, in Exhibit 11-2.

Exhibit 11-2. Examples of Big Ideas in Well-Known Companies

COMPANY	BIG IDEA
Apple	Creativity
BBC	Authoritativeness
British Air	Reassurance
IKEA	Design for the masses
Microsoft	Ubiquity
Nike	Winning
Sony	Perfectionism
Southwest Airlines	Irreverence/Fun
Starbucks	Sociability

This phenomenon isn't restricted to fashionable, highly brand-conscious companies. It applies to workaday businesses like insurance, air cargo, distribution, building products, water utilities, outsourcing companies, paper manufacturers, and law firms.

In organizations, big ideas are most potent when they resonate with larger social changes. As the American magazine *The Nation* wrote in 1943, "There is one thing stronger than all the armies in the world, and that is an idea whose time has come."

Idea-Based Consumer Choices

The world of work is changing into a world of ideas. Ideas are starting to matter more than the organizations that embody them. Instead of Apple versus Microsoft or British Airways versus Virgin, we're moving to a new set of values. Apple stands for creativity, Microsoft for ubiquity; which do you identify with? British Airways offers a kind of reassurance, Virgin a more youthful iconoclasm; which idea can capture more passengers? People are responding to, and engaging with, the ideas that seem right to them, or right *for* them.

"In a way, the emergence of idea-led organizations isn't so surprising," says Jones. "Not when consumers are crying out for organizations to stand for something. Not when investors want organizations to own a magic wellspring of future value. Not when people want to work for organizations that share their own values and priorities.

"And when all these groups of people overlap, it's not so surprising that organizations are looking for one thing to say to all of them. In a world of overcommunication—in a marketplace that's far too noisy—a few organizations are finding bigger, simpler ideas that enable them to rise above the din."

Built to Last...and Last...and Last

So now we have a sense of what constitutes a big idea and what it contributes to a viable enterprise. But why do some big ideas last and others slip off into the sunset?

Jim Collins and Jerry Porras's bestselling book *Built to Last* looks at eighteen of America's most admired companies and shows how important "core ideology," which has many similarities to a big idea, has been for businesses that endure. They conclude that "the existence of a core ideology [is] a primary element in the historical development of visionary companies," defining ideology as a combination of two things—core values and purpose. This core ideology is a constant that is not allowed to change over time.[62] Sound familiar?

Conversely everything else—products, markets, organization structures, and so on—is allowed to change. Indeed, change is strongly and systematically encouraged. A company's growth and success rely heavily on its core values and purpose.

So, the question remains: how do you take a big idea or an ideology and shape it into a lasting brand? Here is where the wisdom of Mike Moser comes into play.

Bottom Line Branding

As a cofounder of the Goldberg Moser O'Neill (GMO) advertising agency, Moser has been involved in creating what he calls "brand road maps" for hundreds of companies. His clients read like a Who's Who of top brands of the last twenty years: Dell Computers, Cisco Systems, Reebok, Apple Computer, and Beringer Wines. He has won more than three hundred national and international advertising awards, including Cannes Lions and five Clios, the highest awards in their field. After helping buy out Chiat/Day, San Francisco, to form GMO, in nine years revenues grew from $95 million to $450 million. Now, he has written the definitive book *United We Brand*.[63]

Brand Road Maps

Having known Mike for many years, I have been well aware of his range of talents as well as his rare ability to synthesize disparate information and make seemingly difficult things simple. He also developed the brand road map for my company, Near Bridge, Inc. The power of his new book rests on how simple he makes the process and how clearly he lays out the four parts of a brand road map:

- *Core Brand Values.* These are the values a brand is built on. They're the foundation of a company and the pillars of every decision made and every message delivered.
- *Core Brand Message.* This is the key message being communicated. All other messages support and add credibility to this message.

- *Brand Personality.* This is the overall tone and attitude used to deliver the message. These traits are the key emotional components that determine whether you have a likeable brand or not.
- *Brand Icons.* These are the tools used to deliver the brand message and brand personality: colors, typefaces, logo, and layouts. They're the elements that make all the marketing materials unique.

When these elements are delivered consistently and cohesively, we have the building blocks—and bottom line profitability—of a long-term, successful brand.

TrendSmart Tip: Brands create customer expectations of quality and consistency, and in so doing create a reputation. A good brand is like a good friend; it inspires trust and resonates with our core values.

Brand Development

Recently I had an online chat with Mike Moser on my monthly show for www.worldwithoutborders.com. As cofounder of Goldberg Moser O'Neill, he helps companies develop their brands by experiencing products and services firsthand and by experiencing people who use and depend on the products firsthand. To set themselves apart, *TrendSmart* companies gather as much knowledge of the marketplace as they can and then use their informed intuition to go for the jugular of whatever niche they're going after.

Informed intuition is more than a hunch. Moser calls it funneling; it's gathering as much information as possible, whether you think it's relevant or not, and then sifting through it unconsciously and consciously to arrive at a solution that is probably 80 percent there.

"Then you start tweaking from the 80 percent," says Moser. On the macro horizon of business and consumer trends as they affect strategies, consumers now tend to think locally and act locally; they are staying with the familiar. Moser sees "more personalization, connection to wider groups of people—not just virtual communities, but stronger individual communities."

Also, from a marketing point of view, he says, "truth will have more of a role." For example, the reality television shows are a trend toward more truthfulness, despite the controlled reality we see on the screen. "We're in an age of image, and everyone is sensitive to, and desensitized by, marketing," he says.

Ever philosophical, Moser quotes David Whyte, saying that "exhaustion isn't cured by rest, but by wholeheartedness. I think that the more companies are wholehearted in what they do and believe in, the less stressed and burned out their employees will be." A related topic is how *TrendSmart* companies should market themselves and/or advertise (i.e., whether or not they should use a traditional approach). Moser feels that there's nothing wrong with the traditional approach that a good dose of "nonentertainment" focus wouldn't cure. "Marketing has become more about being liked than being truthful and relevant," he says.

If you look at what I like to call the "dot-comedy" ads, they offer no information about their products or services; they just make people laugh. Since often their ads reflect the absence of a business model, the last laugh was on them. Ha, ha!…They're gone.

Moser doesn't think Internet-based advertising will be a trend that will just die out soon. He feels that the Internet is the perfect way to talk to someone one on one, and it's the reason, for example, that Dell is so successful. As one of his key accounts early on, Moser helped Dell to see that they were a direct marketing company and

understood one-to-one relationships and accountability to the customer. "Accountability is the key," he says.

Moser advises leaders to ask whether their businesses are relevant.
"They should ask if they can make their relationships with their customers deeper. Like a friend," he says. "People have always voted with
their wallets. Now they're looking to vote with their hearts."

"Topics like ecology, wastefulness, relevance, and the like are
entering the consumer's buying vocabulary," Moser observes. The
customer-service implications of following your heart "hearken back
to personalization. Direct marketing. Face to face. Treat a customer
like you would a friend. If you like them for more than their wallet,
let them know. If you have a good idea for them, let them know."

The Power of Trend Analysis

The power of good information, early on, has never been greater than
in uncertain times like today. The power of trend analysis comes, in
part, from its role in the creation of big ideas. If you know where
things are heading, you can test the mettle of a potentially big idea
against the prospect of the trends. Further, once you have a big idea
in place, you can continually match the idea to the emerging trends
and modify products and services accordingly.

The combination of good trend information, the application of
that information to a big idea, and a strong brand road map that
would make Mike Moser proud helps shape a formula for success.
Here is how this works. For the moment, let's assume that you know
your trends, and you have the big idea. Let's also assume that you
have created a brand road map. Now what?

**TrendSmart Tip: The blending of *TrendSmart* information, a
big idea, the brand road map, and the ability to deliver on the
promise of the brand is the key to sustainable success.**

Well, this is the point at which we enter the domain of implementation, of consistently "delivering on the promise of the brand," as they say in business school. Good trend analysis, which contributes to a big idea with a great brand road map, is of little use if you cannot take it to the marketplace. Properly done, a formula for sustainable success looks like Exhibit 11-3.

Exhibit 11-3. An Equation for Effective Trend Implementation

$$T + \frac{Bi + Br}{D} = S^2$$

Where: T = Trends, properly understood; plus a

Bi = Big idea; plus a

Br = Brand road map; divided by

D = Delivering on the promise of the idea and brand; equals

S^2 = Sustainable Success.

The equation in Exhibit 11-3 is best understood as a continuing process, for out of successes often come the anomalies that are the seeds of new emergent trends. On and on and on it goes. Guided by this equation, the journey is made simpler and easier.

We have looked at trends and big ideas and brand road maps to better understand their utility. It remains now to examine some factors that affect the ability to deliver on the promise of the brand.

TrendSmart **Tips**

- Good organizations need both a richly compelling big idea and a clever, evolving brand road map.
- A business model targets some way of making money, but a big idea engages people...so a good business plan should be coupled with a big idea.
- Effective brand-building companies create depth of engagement, which means appealing to customers at levels other than the purely rational...and this intimacy is far more effective for organizations than vision or brand.
- Brands create customer expectations of quality and consistency, and in so doing create a reputation. A good brand is like a good friend; it inspires trust and resonates with our core values.
- The blending of *TrendSmart* information, a big idea, the brand road map, and the ability to deliver on the promise of the brand is the key to sustainable success.

Chapter 12

Selective Service

Where the Best Customers Get the Best Service

⊕ ⊕ ⊕

*"No man would listen to you talk if he
didn't know it was his turn next."*
—*Ed Howe, nineteenth-century journalist*

In today's business environment, the reality is that a relatively small percentage of your customers generate a disproportionately large amount of your business. The 80/20 principle states that 20 percent of your customers account for 80 percent of your business. Companies today need to reexamine their sales and marketing strategies and align them with emerging market and customer trends. Because the most successful companies have at least bifurcated their sales strategies, separating the best prospects and the loyal customers from the rest, I refer to this emerging trend as "selective service." Knowing which customers to spoil and which to leave for the competition is one of the challenges savvy leaders face today.

TrendSmart Tip: Customer service follows the 80/20 principle: a small percentage of your customers generate a disproportionately large amount of your business—so make sure you're meeting the needs of your core customers.

"It's simple," says Guy Kawasaki, CEO and chairman of garage.com and former Apple chief evangelist. "Sell to people who want your product; ignore those who don't. I spent years trying to get people to buy into Macintosh. We were selling a dream of how the world might become a better place....It took me a while to learn that you can't convert atheists."[64]

The *TrendSmart* leader understands that the emerging trend toward selective service is developing in tandem with that of mass customization (discussed in chapter 9). In both trends, there is a common thread of individualizing the relationship with the customer. Once you know your customers well, it is much easier to anticipate their needs and offer the specialized services that will win their business.

Chief Customer Officer

The rise of CRM—customer relationship management—over the last decade has signaled the increasing sophistication of gathering and using pertinent customer data. The technology is now in place to know a great deal about a single customer at any single point in time. Knowing thy customer has never been more vital, detailed, or virtual than it is today, thanks to advanced computer software, "cookies" (customer identifiers placed on your hard drive by Web servers), detailed "data mining," and access to unprecedented amounts of public information via a few simple clicks. You can know the habits, preferences, and patterns of every customer, and thereby develop a clear profile of how to best serve them.

So complex has CRM become that experts advocate employing specialists at the senior levels of a company. Well-known consultant Patricia Seybold suggests appointing a CCO—chief customer officer—to oversee the use of information about your customers and to integrate all of the information that you have about each customer into a comprehensive customer profile.[65]

TrendSmart Tip: With today's sophisticated database technology, it's possible to know the habits, preferences, and patterns of every one of your customers—so make sure you do!

Turkeys, Thieves, and Diamonds: Reward Your Best Customers

Good consumer information helps shape good strategy, and good customer-service strategy often runs contrary to conventional wisdom. For example, several years ago New York's Green Hills Farms grocery store turned industry habits upside down when it organized marketing promotions around customers, rather than products. Using, among other things, an innovative frequent-shopper program, Green Hill was able to reward its best customers, ensure their continued patronage, and reap higher gross margins. Susan Greco tells us how in her article "The Best Little Grocery Store in America."

In an industry notorious for bone-thin margins, Green Hills's CEO Gary Hawkins was frustrated with the industry practice of giving away turkeys below cost to anyone who walked in the door at holiday time. Thinking to himself "there must be a better way," he made a revolutionary decision: Green Hills would stop helping the customers they referred to as "thieves" (bargain-thirsty, store-hopping, coupon-wielding customers with no loyalty except to their own wallets) and start rewarding its highest-spending repeat customers. Hawkins launched Green Hills' first "Great Gobbler Giveaway," a daring and risky initiative for the little store. In order to be given a turkey at Thanksgiving, customers were required to commit to spending at least $500 at the store over the ten preceding weeks. The result? The "thieves" went elsewhere, and Green Hills then realized higher profits on the same level of sales to their remaining high-end customer base.

Today, Green Hills has a wildly successful and highly respected frequent-buyer program replete with creative perks for top-spending "Diamond" customers. Examples include $25-off coupons for the garden shop in the spring and "restock your fridge" coupons after a tornado or power outage. Further, a designated "new customer manager" takes you on a personal tour of the store. With this personalized attention, top customers not only returned consistently but also spent a few more dollars on average than before.

The loyalty of Green Hills' best customers has paid off as six rival supermarkets entered its sales area in recent years—one just across the Green Hills parking lot. When two competitors moved into the neighborhood on the same day, Hawkins and his managers knew just what to do. They appealed for support to their most loyal Diamond customers. Turning to the customer database, director of information services Lisa Piron generated a list of best customers by department. Then she composed a letter thanking each of them for being a good customer and enclosed a gift certificate for a gift basket from the customer's favorite department. Department managers personally handed the baskets out. Hawkins reports that the store not only held its own against the new competition but even gained sales and a few return customers via that promotion.

TrendSmart Tip: Stop rewarding _all_ of your customers because many of them are bargain-thirsty, store-hopping, coupon-wielding customers with no loyalty to you; instead, reward your _best_ customers—and watch your business grow!

Green Hills retains better than 96 percent of its Diamond customers each year. Its overall year-to-year customer-retention rate is 80 percent. While most stores look at product shrinkage or how much inventory the store loses because of theft or damage, Green Hills looks at _customer_ shrinkage—and not just _any_ customers, but the high-end customers who can most affect its bottom line.

Before instituting Green Hills' customer loyalty program, says Hawkins, "It was like operating blind." With the success and notoriety of Green Hills, Hawkins now travels the world helping other retailers see the light. He even self-published a book on loyalty marketing. Now, reports Greco, "The store no longer wastes time and precious marketing dollars chasing folks who come in to pick the cheap cherries and pluck the underpriced turkeys."[66]

No Duping

In selling, honesty really is the best policy. But in a world of slick advertising and instant branding (see chapter 11, "Reputation Creation"), honesty can fall prey to art, clarity to flash and glitz.

"My partner and I are just a couple of regular idiots who happen to run a company," says Tom Scott, cofounder and CEO of Nantucket Nectars. "People often ask me, 'How do you sell to Generation X?'…The best way to sell to anyone is to tell it like it is—which sounds simple but which apparently isn't. For instance, look at the boys in Detroit. I'm always amazed by how they sell cars. Instead of grounding their sales pitch in the benefits of their cars, they talk about lifestyle and being cool—or about limited-slip differential and rack-and-pinion steering. No one knows what those things mean! People know when they're being duped. So the best way to sell to them is not to try to dupe them."[67]

Efficiency Is *Not* Service!

To provide great service today we must think differently, and we must not confuse efficiency with service. Efficiency is now merely a given—the price of entry. It is only through service *excellence* that you gain the competitive advantage in the global marketplace. The challenge is to strike the right balance, customer to customer, between efficiency and service. But how do you do that?

For starters, take customer service seriously. Inattention, disdain, and routine phrases all paint a picture of poor service and leave the customer underwhelmed. I recall seeing a cartoon twenty years ago showing two customers standing in front of a small-town bank. One explains to the other, "I prefer small banks; the indifference is more personal." Today, even personalized indifference will not be tolerated.

TrendSmart Tip: Don't focus on *efficiency* when serving customers; instead, focus on *excellence*.

The modern prosumer requires more, because as Gary Hamel says in *Leading the Revolution*, we live in a world of "rising expectations and diminishing returns." To get more, we have to do more. We have to go beyond the obvious and the traditional; we have to add some new tools to the toolbox; and we have to break a few rules in the process. As I look at the last decade's most respected (e.g., Rubbermaid, Merck), fastest-growing (Gap, Sun Microsystems), and most customer-focused (Nordstrom, Ritz-Carlton) companies, I find that they have much in common. As Tolstoy once wrote: "All happy families resemble one another."

Give Your Customers What They Want

Few industries are under more scrutiny than the airlines. This was true before September 11, and has only been exacerbated since then. Nonetheless, in some areas such as customer service, the link between profitability and quality service remains. American industry leader Gordon Bethune, CEO of Continental Airlines, explains how he brought Continental from the brink of bankruptcy to its front-running position: "If you take the cheese off the pizza, you can make a pizza so cheap that nobody will eat it. You can make an airline so cheap nobody will fly it. We just put the cheese back on. We need to listen to what customers want and will pay for. Passengers will pay for clean airplanes; they will pay for reliable baggage service. We became profitable when we increased our service."[68]

The airline industry certainly has operated a two-tiered service system for decades, first class and coach, with supposedly clear value-added differences between the two to warrant the price differential. But when Bethune examined the two classes of service, he found many anomalies, even on seemingly mundane levels. "The coach meals have better candy—those chocolate turtles—than the first-class meal. I asked why we can't have them in first class, and they said the other ones are more elegant. I said forget that, people want something that's good," says Bethune.

Putting the Right Price on Service

Part of understanding the nuances of selective service is knowing how you establish a value and price for your services. Whether you have dual pricing like the airlines, one price for all products, or as many pricing options as there are customers, every business model eventually has to make some pricing choices, and those choices may be affected by that great equalizer, the customer's wallet.

In some companies, the pricing schemes include a certain percentage of products being used as "loss leaders," products on which they are willing to lose money in order to sell other, more profitable items. The risk here is the consumer who buys only loss leaders. On the other hand, with "bait and switch" pricing, where the actual selection is minimal at the price quoted, the risk is that the prosumer will likely see this as deceptive at best, or cause for taking business to a competitor at worst.

I am reminded of the humorous story about a little boy who walked into an ice cream store and asked for a scoop of pistachio ice cream. When the owner told him it would cost a dollar, the boy said that the store across the street charged only seventy-nine cents.

"So why don't you buy it there?" asked the owner.

"Because they are out of pistachio," the boy replied.

"Well," said the owner, "if I were out of pistachio, I'd charge seventy-nine cents, too."

The ice cream store example adds *availability* to the equation, in addition to pricing and service.

Some industries, such as fashion and cosmetics, attempt to control pricing by creating a sense of status or scarcity. Though they may still emphasize service, their pricing model yields extremely high margins paid by high-end customers.

Keep Up with Your Customers' Preferences

There are times, too, when selective service is based upon the evolving relationship itself. As times change, so does consumer behavior, often in surprising ways. As one who tracks trends for a living, I am acutely aware of this. One example is that according to a recent Home Depot/Yankelovich Partners study, women picked home improvement over shopping or cooking as their preferred household leisure activity. Thirty-seven percent of women say they would prefer to spend their weekend leisure time working on a home-improvement or outdoor project, 28 percent prefer shopping at a mall, and 25 percent prefer cooking or baking. Thirty-three percent of men say they prefer spending their leisure time doing an outdoor home-improvement project, 15 percent like shopping at a mall, 12 percent like cooking or baking, 16 percent would rather do an indoor home-improvement project, and 21 percent chose none of the above. Surprisingly, 54 percent of women say they were in the process of planning a home-improvement project, compared with 51 percent of men.[69] So the conventional stereotypes of home repair and improvement as a man's world may need to be revisited.

Consequently, if you were a *TrendSmart* CEO of Home Depot, or the local hardware store, you might well alter your displays and floor plans and product offerings to make them more interesting to your female customers. The layout of the store, the height of items on the shelves, the color schemes—all of these things should be selectively altered for your changing customer base.

Know What Motivates Your Customer

Knowing the intricacies of your clients' tastes and buying habits is part of the big, selective picture. An often-missed element is understanding what motivates them, knowing *why* they buy what they buy. "Clients don't really care about *your* stuff. They care about *their* stuff," says Mark Bozzini, CEO of Linkexchange Inc. "You have to be able to put your finger on what motivates your customer."[70]

TrendSmart Tip: Have multiple service strategies…something for the best customers that keeps them feeling special and valued. Do not take them for granted, ever.

Bozzoni then tells a story to illustrate. "I walked into one account, and I could tell immediately that the owner was having a bad day. With something like sixty thousand items in his store, he had more than two hundred vendors vying for his attention. This guy looked at me and said, 'As far as I'm concerned, your stuff doesn't sell, and I'd just as soon not have it on my shelf.' Standing there, I had three thoughts: I need an immediate career change; I'm never going to make it as a salesman; and I have to figure out a way to make this sale. I went to where my products were displayed and—not knowing that this was illegal (I was nonunion)—started to rearrange the bottles on the shelves. After an hour, I brought him over to show him what I had done. He screamed at me for fiddling with his shelf space, but he finally agreed that my arrangement looked much better than the previous one."

Going Out of Your Way to Help Customers

In the restaurant industry, we see many examples of selective service at work. Consider this story from Red Robin restaurants:

> A gentleman entered the restaurant to enjoy another great Novi/Town Center Red Robin dining experience in Novi, Michigan. His server, Kerrie Swanson, noticed that the guest was having difficulty reading the menu—he was recovering from eye surgery. Kerrie sat down and proceeded to read the menu to the guest, guiding him through his order. The man was very touched. It was a small task, but it meant much to this guest in need. Unbridled acts need not be large; just showing you care makes you big in the eyes of our guests! Thank you, Kerrie, for your unbridled spirit! We're always looking for team members who have an unbridled passion for life.[71]

There are many lessons to be learned from this example:

• Selective service is one-size-fits-one service.

- Selective service anticipates customer needs.
- Selective service offers value-added elements to differentiate itself from competitors.

Kerri Swanson's selective service, no doubt, left a favorable impression with her customer. In a world of episodic customer loyalty, my guess is she added something special enough that her customer will return.

Do Your Own Thing...On a Small Scale

We are all looking for that little edge and advantage today. As the future becomes more and more difficult to predict, there is an increased desire for formulaic answers. It's no wonder that consulting companies have profited for years from implementing TQM, CRM, process reengineering, and similar initiatives for dealing with business uncertainties.

But in the world of selective service, "doing your own thing" in nontraditional ways, on a small scale, every chance you get, also creates a positive and powerful impact. Exhibit 12-1 offers other examples of great customer service.

Exhibit 12-1. Examples of Great Customer Service

- A waiter at the Sugar Beach Resort in Mauritius comes to work each day with a thermometer in his pocket. On the way to the restaurant, he takes the temperature of the ocean water and the swimming pool. As he pours coffee and clears plates during breakfast, he joyfully tells guests exactly how warm and enjoyable their swimming will be that day.
- A room-service attendant noticed a guest from Germany reading Goethe during her stay. He got coaching from a colleague and learned a poem in German by

heart. A few days later he delivered dinner to her room and recited the poem proudly for her enjoyment.

- A sales clerk at Nordstrom sold a man a new pair of shoes. Measuring his feet, the clerk discovered that the man's right foot was size 9.5 and his left foot was a smaller 9.0. The clerk sold the man the shoes he needed to achieve a perfect fit: one size 9.5 and the other 9.0. Nobody knows what the clerk did with the remaining mismatched shoes, but the customer's loyalty to Nordstrom was secured.

- A furniture maker in Malaysia gives its "Corporate Warrior Award" to staff members for extraordinary deeds. A customer returned one large furniture item and selected another. A partial refund was due, but the customer planned to leave the country that very night. One staff member offered to process the refund paperwork on the same day. At 8:15 P.M., he arrived at the customer's house with the refund check in hand...and a small cake with "Bon Voyage!" written across the top.

Exhibit 12-1 comes from Ron Kaufman, and in typical Kaufman fashion, he then asks all of us: "What is 'your thing'? Is it the personal note you attach to documents? Is it the enthusiastic tone in your voice on the phone? Is it your pride in teaching customers or colleagues something new? Is it as simple as the colorful clothes you wear, the magazine and newspaper articles you share with others, or your passion for indoor plants that makes the whole office come alive? Whatever it is that turns you on, turn 'your thing' to the advantage and enjoyment of others."

TrendSmart Tips

- Customer service follows the 80/20 principle: a small percentage of your customers generate a disproportionately large amount of your business—so make sure you're meeting the needs of your core customers.
- With today's sophisticated database technology, it's possible to know the habits, preferences, and patterns of every one of your customers—so make sure you do!
- Stop rewarding *all* of your customers because many of them are bargain-thirsty, store-hopping, coupon-wielding customers with no loyalty to you; instead, reward your *best* customers—and watch your business grow!
- Don't focus on *efficiency* when serving customers; instead, focus on *excellence*.
- Have multiple service strategies…something for the best customers that keeps them feeling special and valued. Do not take them for granted, ever.

Chapter 13

Episodic Loyalty

Where Customers and Employees Have Multiple, Fleeting Loyalties

⊕ ⊕ ⊕

"Customers are loyal right up until the second that
somebody offers them better service."

—Jeff Bezos, CEO of Amazon.com

Gone is the era of lifelong customer loyalty to a brand or product and single-track careers at one company. Gone are the days of the whole family banking in one place, now that lenders solicit you via phone, email, and the Web. Gone is building a long-term relationship with any one physician in today's age of HMOs. And long gone are the days when a "long-term commitment" meant decades, not weeks. That's the sobering, tough news.

The good news is that loyalty is alive and well…it just has a much shorter life span! For example, at eighteen you may buy a used Chevy; at twenty-seven, a sporty Miata; at thirty-three, after baby number one comes along, a Ford Explorer; at fifty, it's back to the Chevy brand, maybe this time a Corvette in a midlife-crisis buying frenzy. If nothing else, loyalty is *episodic.*

Today, the retail customer is more fickle, yet more desirous of choices than ever. We want 116 cable television channels; 480 mortgage-rate options online; and Thai, Italian, sushi, and burrito restaurants within two blocks. Choice is the name of the game, and once the choice is made, we remain loyal to it—until we make the next choice.

TrendSmart Tip: Customer loyalty is alive and well, but it has a much shorter life span; today's customer loyalty is *episodic.*

In some industries, the turnover of customers is a substantial part of their business-planning process. The mobile-phone industry, for example, has an annual churn rate of around 35 percent. This is a high enough figure to start with, but additional factors serve to exacerbate the problem. As most handsets are heavily subsidized and network access costs are swallowed, there is little or no return on investment (ROI) for the first two years. Loss of customers therefore means loss of both revenue and investment.[72]

Customer Loyalty at Risk…and Recovered

Episodic loyalty is risky business. As the following three stories illustrate, you can put your customer relationship at risk very easily, and you can recover customer loyalty as well.

"Every month I ship packages to customers around the world," says Ron Kaufman. "My favorite courier company has a 'bonus program' to encourage and reward customer loyalty. Two years ago the program offered a cash discount for volume shipping. Last year the program was changed to provide shopping and dining vouchers instead of discounts."

At the end of the year, Kaufman realized that he had never received a single dining or shopping voucher. "I contacted the courier company and was told, 'Since you already get a special corporate rate, you are no longer eligible for the bonus vouchers.' The company never mentioned this to me when they changed the terms of the bonus program. But on the phone the representative said, 'But if you like, your shipping volume is high enough that we can increase your corporate discount rate from 26 percent to 40 percent.'"

That was odd, because his shipping volume had been fairly consistent for several years. Kaufman then asked, "When did I qualify for a 40 percent discount rate?"

The representative replied, "About twenty-four months ago."

That was upsetting. For two years, he had qualified for a lower shipping rate, but the courier company never told him. Then they disqualified him from their new bonus program and never informed him.

Kaufman then told the representative, rightly: "My loyalty to your company is at risk. You folks need to do some recovery, and fast."

The representative's response was gradual and measured, with no personalized effort to reclaim lost goodwill. "I asked her twice in writing for the name and email address of her general manager," he said. "She simply ignored my requests."

If you were in his shoes, you'd do what he did: open a new account with their competition.

As a vendor, the last thing you want is for your most loyal customers to learn that your promotions offer better deals to new customers than to them or that they have qualified for volume discounts for months without having been notified. You may think you can charge them more for a while and only change "if they find out."

But there's a problem with that approach: when they do find out, they will not want to be your customer anymore.

"Your loyal customers deserve your best available deals and discounts. Don't ever take them for granted. Do a rigorous review of your special pricing, packages, and promotions. Make sure you offer your best customers the best you have to offer," says Kaufman.

Loyal customers are worth retaining. If something happens and your loyal customer feels burned, abused, or taken for granted, you better hustle to set things right! Just "fixing the problem" won't be enough. Short-term costs, effort, or embarrassment are a small price to pay for long-term purchases, profits, and support.

A second story has a happier ending. Kaufman sends thousands of audio and video learning systems overseas. "I recently had a complaint from a customer about a videotape that 'skipped' during playback," said Kaufman. "I thought it was an oddity and immediately replaced the tape. But the next month another complaint arrived about the same situation. I took action."

The video-duplication company apologized profusely and promised immediate replacement, explaining that this problem was limited to a small number of videocassettes from a single spool of defective tape. Kaufman removed the remaining inventory—a few hundred pieces—and sent the tapes back.

He got a message from the company offering to replace only "verified bad tapes." What was he supposed to do, watch every tape and look out for those that "skip"? Or wait for his customers to notice the problem and complain, and then exchange those tapes one at a time? Of course not. The better course of action was to simply—and quickly—replace them all. He told them so in a follow-up message.

To their credit, the duplication company responded to the second message in an entirely appropriate manner. They agreed to replace all the tapes at no charge. They also promised to put extraordinary care into future duplications to ensure the highest quality standards. That's a smart business move. It guarantees more business and fosters a modicum of loyalty.

Kaufman's third story brings new insight. Many companies treat "customer service" as a necessary evil, an afterthought, a department only needed if mistakes and problems arise. This viewpoint is best reflected in the common statement: "No news is good news!"

Harvard's Theodore Levitt once said, "One of the surest signs of a bad or declining relationship with a customer is the absence of complaints. Nobody is ever that satisfied, especially not over an extended period of time. The customer is either not being candid or is not being contacted." In other words, when it comes to customers, no news is bad news.

If you have happy customers and you do not actively give them a chance to tell you, you lose one of the strongest opportunities to increase customer loyalty. The need to be internally consistent is a driving force in shaping future behavior. In other words, if customers tell you how and why they are happy, they are very likely to repeat the behavior that caused them such satisfaction, which was doing business with you! And what if you have an unhappy customer? Who would you rather they tell all about it—you, or your prospects, competitors, and other customers?

TrendSmart Tip: In customer service, "no news" is *not* "good news." If your customers aren't giving you feedback on what they think of your service, it could be because they're going elsewhere for their business. Make sure you check in with your customers to find out how you're doing.

A few years ago, I chose Singapore Airlines for a flight to Singapore, primarily because I was told that Delta would apply these miles to my frequent-flyer account with them. After submitting my ticket for mileage credit, I received a letter listing restrictions and acceptable fare types that disqualified my trip from eligibility in the program. In a second letter, I made explicit the extent of my annual travel and the basis of my choice to fly Singapore Air. Five days later, I received a letter from Kathleen Kozai, market planning assistant for Singapore Airlines, stating "You do qualify for mileage accumulation for the fare basis you had purchased....I will rectify this situation with Delta Air Lines." As a result, I continue to fly on both airlines with true—and episodic—loyalty.

Employee Loyalty

There are many similarities between the trend toward episodic loyalty amongst customers as well as among employees. We will see more on how to attract and retain employees in part 3. When we discuss the trend toward "paid volunteers," employees often behave like customers, echoing the words of blues singer Tracy Chapman, who sang "Give me one reason to stay here, and I'll turn right back around."

"I've always felt that companies pay lip service to their employees," says Kelley Robertson, national sales trainer of the retail division of Sony of Canada. "Employers can say that family is important, but often they're referring to the boss's family—not mine."[73]

TrendSmart leaders understand employee episodic loyalty soberly and do not place a value judgment on it. Rather, they take it as a strategic "given" of today's workplace. Employees, they understand, can be very devoted, productive, and committed to their jobs, but not for all that long. Knowing this, *TrendSmart* managers can plan a productivity curve of three to four years per employee. They have to get their people up to speed quickly, keep them motivated, and assume that they have a short attention span and will move on.

TrendSmart Tip: Employee loyalty is becoming increasingly like customer loyalty—and it's not something that managers can take for granted anymore.

At many companies, the growth of a project-based culture is a fitting adaptation to the realities of the times: keep people engaged for short time lengths, then cycle them into something else. In that way, you can keep top talent longer within a company so long as they are not doing the same old, same old.

Three out of four Americans are dissatisfied with or fundamentally disconnected from their jobs, according to a recent *Gallup Management Journal* survey. Matthew Boyle quotes a disgruntled dot-com employee, who prefers to remain anonymous: "The closest I get to job satisfaction is a thirty-minute nap in my car after lunch."[74] Such bitterness often echoes throughout a workplace.

Boyle continues his analysis of job satisfaction and worker-friendly companies: "Granted, workers have been miserable for centuries—but is the joy of working gone for good? Not by a long shot. The demise of companies like Kozmo, Pets.com, and their ilk didn't kill workplace fun any more than their arrival created it. Rather, the dot-coms accelerated and took mainstream a trend that began well before anyone had heard of Yahoo. Traditional companies scrambled to provide a more employee-friendly atmosphere, as they figured the best way to keep their staff…was to emulate the Silicon Valley culture." After all, would you not do at least that much to retain a customer? "The dot-coms caused a lot of fury around keeping people engaged," says Sherry Perley, senior vice president of human resources at Snapple.

"I told you so" critics of the dot-com movement now argue that a worker-friendly culture precipitated the dot-com demise. "The stuffier side of establishment America is now backlashing and making fun of what was occurring in these dot-com environments," says

Nigel Morris, president and COO of credit-card giant Capital One (which itself is still committed to fun). The dot-com culture as well as the business model is under indictment.

"Rather than replace one extreme (emulation) with another (rejection)," says Boyle, "a better approach is to blend what worked in dot-com land with your existing culture. Casual dress, flextime, and telecommuting are three examples." If these options are appropriate to your company culture and your local employees, use them. As Boyle notes, "All existed before the Internet craze (Levi's began its casual-dress crusade in 1992, and Hewlett-Packard rolled out flex-time way back in 1973)."

"Our prognostication is that we'll see blended cultures going forward," says Joan Caruso, managing director of organizational effectiveness at the Ayers Group. "Indeed," Boyle concludes, "in a recent survey of business school students by academic consulting firm Universum, most respondents said they desired an informal work environment but at an established organization."

Serial Monogamy

There is really nothing all that new about episodic loyalty. It is a phenomenon that anthropologists first spotted more than a century ago in cultures that practiced "serial monogamy," a sequence of time-limited but devoted social commitments. Much like dating one person at a time, when that runs its course, it is a free market. Customers and employees are much the same—committed for a while, guiltless when moving on.

Today, smart companies that capitalize on this are at a distinct advantage. They understand that if you have a customer's loyalty for only so long, make the most of it. Make the "relationship" such that at the very least the customer has had a good experience with your product and brand so they will return to you at a later date. Buy that Chevy now. Buy another years later.

According to Christopher Selland, vice president of The Yankee Group's e-Business Strategies Research and Consulting Group, "Customers want to be loyal, but companies need to give them the opportunity to do so."[75]

Early Warning Signs

As more and more people are becoming disillusioned with their jobs faster and faster, and with job "loyalty" now an archaic, nostalgic concept, how do you know when it is time to go? How can a manager assess the early warning signs of a worker who is dying on the job? The early signs are easy to see, if you are looking. For example, a change in time of arrival, withdrawing from usual conversations, more complaining, more whining, a more "distant" attitude, and changes in pace of work and amount of "passion," too, will signal a shift. Of course, finding monster.com on the computer screen is a clue, too!

Sometimes an employee may dislike a project, a certain person, or a new assignment. When there is a *pattern* to his or her dislikes, then a manager should pay attention. Many of the early warning signs of job disengagement are similar to early signs of depression—and for good reason, as they are quite often similar. People become disillusioned with their jobs faster today, for a variety of reasons. Things change so quickly these days that jobs have to change, too. Sometimes the job shifts are for the better; sometimes not.

TrendSmart Tip: Watch for changes in employee work habits to determine whether one of your staff is burned out or ready to move on.

Often, though, it is not the "job;" it is a problem with a person, a boss, a climate, or a company "culture." Employers should build relationships with their employees in much the same way they build relationships with customers.

In a tight labor market, jobs are plentiful. But, when things shift and it is more difficult to find work, employees will need skills in compromise, negotiation, etc. Today, if you are unhappy, you leave and may not find other work. But, like marrying, at some point you have to know where your commitments are.

Also, keep in mind that it is *not* human resources' job nor that of the manager to look for signs of a "dying staffer"—someone who is burning out or losing interest. It is *everyone's* job. Often we delegate the human side of business to the human-resources department. Like delegating creativity to the art department, or cost cutting to the accounting department, it is too little too late too often.

Keep in mind that an ambiguous employee is not necessarily a sure sign that the working relationship is over. It may be in trouble, but not over. In some instances, ambiguity is a good thing, especially self-reflective ambiguity. We all have to look inside ourselves every day. We have to ask ourselves tough questions. We have to understand *why* we feel ambiguity on the job. We have to know our options. We have to have a sense that there is a future for us. We have to feel challenged and productive, like we are making a contribution. If we do not feel these things, the ambiguity will not remain ambiguous for long, right?

I use the word "feel" intentionally, because deciding to stay or leave a job—or a relationship, or a city—is emotional. So this is a case where you do benefit from trusting your feelings. A good way to not have regrets is to leave with doors open.

You can always "reinvent" yourself in lieu of firing yourself. You can be self-employed and feel just as ambiguous as any employee. Though it is easier to change job descriptions while self-employed, few do. I have found that self-employed people have *more* trouble recognizing when they are dead on the job than those at big companies. It is human nature. There is no human-resources department for the self-employed.

Finally, keep in mind that employee loyalty affects every aspect of work. Certainly how long one works at a place is highly affected by one's sense of loyalty. These days, people—call them customers or employees—are fickle. To paraphrase Yogi Berra, loyalty, like the future, just ain't what it used to be. Loyalty is a *value*, and our values guide our behavior. Loyalty is from the heart—not the head or the wallet. Some are loyal about some things (for example, family or relationships), while not too loyal in other areas (for example, jobs, products, politics, etc.). Everyone is unique. But I do see much less loyalty to companies than I did even two years ago.

Employees and managers need to recognize that it's time to move on from a job when the job starts affecting their health or their loved ones. Then you know you have waited too long, and it is time to move on. On the other hand, it is good to be thankful too, to be *alive* on the job and to know it. There are cycles to things as well. So this week you may hate work, and next week you may like it much better. Celebrate the good times; correct the bad times.

TrendSmart Tips

- Customer loyalty is alive and well, but it has a much shorter life span; today's customer loyalty is *episodic.*
- In customer service, "no news" is *not* "good news." If your customers aren't giving you feedback on what they think of your service, it could be because they're going elsewhere for their business. Make sure you check in with your customers to find out how you're doing.
- Employee loyalty is becoming increasingly like customer loyalty— and it's not something that managers can take for granted anymore.
- Watch for changes in employee work habits to determine whether one of your staff is burned out or ready to move on.

PART THREE

The TrendSmart Employee

Pieces of a Puzzle

We have now looked at several emerging trends in companies and customers that every *TrendSmart* leader needs to understand fully, commend to memory, and use in combination in order to gain an advantage in the marketplace in uncertain times. We turn now to the third and final piece of the *TrendSmart* puzzle: the *TrendSmart* employee. Someone, after all, will have to follow the leaders and serve the customer.

In the following eight chapters, you will gain needed insight into how to motivate workers and make your workforce more productive. Again, the fine art of *TrendSmart* leadership is to now juxtapose what you know about companies and customers with what you will shortly know about employees as well.

Chapter 14

Paid Volunteers
Where Workers Work Because They *Want* To

⊕ ⊕ ⊕

"What thou lovest well is thy true heritage."

—*Ezra Pound, poet*

A persistent trend in the emerging values in the workforce has been labeled "free-agent nation." Seeing themselves as paid volunteers, free agents work because they *want* to work at a particular job, at a particular point in time, for particular personal reasons. Even in tough times, they make short-range plans and commitments. "One of the greatest lessons," observes W. Michael Cox, chief economist of the Dallas Federal Reserve Bank, "is that the secret to growth is losing jobs."[76] According to the Bureau of Labor Statistics, 8.2 million people currently work as independent contractors.[77] In fact, despite all the noise about the United States becoming a nation of free agents, the current number of independent contractors—slightly more than 6 percent of the total workforce—has remained practically unchanged since 1996.

To free agents, moving from job to job is often seen as a badge of honor. They are self-sufficient and perhaps best understood as sole proprietorships, constantly reinventing and marketing themselves via a set of "virtual assets."

TrendSmart Tip: Employees today see themselves as "free agents," because they *want* to work at a particular job, at a particular point in time, for particular personal reasons.

Free agents are not motivated by conventional incentives, because even when working in large companies, they see themselves more as entrepreneurs, pursuing a series of interesting jobs. Some define loyalty as working hard for a company today, but not forever. They prefer high-intensity, short-duration assignments. They want pay based on performance, not longevity. They want mentoring, but they don't care as much about a clear career path. And they don't see anything wrong with job-hopping.

TrendSmart Tip: Engage employees by giving them high-intensity, short-duration project assignments, working in changeable teams.

According to Bill Breen, "These workers say to themselves, I want a place where there are lots of opportunities because my experience will enable me to take on many different jobs and projects. I *might* decide to have a long tenure at one company, but my assumption going into the job is that my connection to work is insecure and temporary—partly because that's the nature of the new economy, and partly because I have watched my family members get laid off, and I know that corporations aren't loyal."[78]

Business writer Dave Murphy offers some salient observations. "It's a new generation of workers," says Murphy. "But it's not Generation X."

(I find "Gen X" too vague a term to be predictive, but I will use research by others because some points are applicable to this chapter.) Gen Xers are no more likely to emphasize those qualities than people in their 50s, according to a survey by Interim Services Inc. and Louis Harris & Associates. The national survey of 1,001 adults says 22 percent of workers are 'emergent,' people with those types of attitudes, while 29 percent think traditionally, emphasizing job security and a clear career path."[79]

TrendSmart Tip: Pay employees based on their performance, not their longevity with the company.

The remaining 49 percent of respondents are described by Interim's CEO, Ray Marcy, as "migrating," people with some traditional values and some emergent ones. He believes that workers are changing toward the emergent mind-set of wanting "career security" instead of traditional job security.

"Although age and experience made little difference in the ratio of emergent workers to traditional ones, a couple of demographic factors did. Those with college degrees or annual salaries of more than $50,000 were far more likely to be emergent employees than traditional ones," observes Murphy.

The "emergent" workers in the survey work hard, take risks, work well in teams, and are project oriented. On the other hand, they can work too hard for too long and burn out, they can be loners while on a team, myopic while engaged in a major initiative, and feel "entitled" to special attention when generosity and sharing would be useful.

TrendSmart Tip: Mentor your employees and allow them to pursue unconventional career paths within the company. There's no such thing as a straight "corporate ladder" anymore.

Free agents know their strengths and weaknesses, and therefore work to improve their skills, constantly reconfiguring and repackaging themselves. Free agents understand volunteerism and a work ethic in which work is not what defines the person. What you *do* and who you *are* are increasingly disparate and separable things.

What Makes GenX Tick?

Understanding what motivates productivity is increasingly important. Nowhere is this more prevalent than it is for managers with substantial numbers of employees from Generation X. In fact, Exhibit 14-1 offers some examples of how many *TrendSmart* managers have made special efforts to understand their GenXers and what makes them productive.

Exhibit 14-1. Examples of Companies that Are Embracing the GenX Workforce

- *Mervyn's department store.* "All we were exposed to was the (images of the) earring in the nose, snowboards, and baggy clothing," says Deborah Gatti, senior training specialist for Mervyn's department stores says of GenX work. "We've had to train our culture about the great things about these folks, and their shortcomings and how we can support them."[80]
- *Sandia National Laboratories.* "The GenX age group does come to the workplace with different expectations and experiences," says Don Blanton, human-resources director at Sandia National Laboratories, which has recently revised key management-training programs to include lessons on what makes Generation X tick.[81]
- *Pixar Animation Studios.* The work environment is especially important to GenXers. One animator created a Hawaiian tiki lodge; another built a secret, '60s-style "love nest," complete with disco lights in an adjoining utility closet. "Where you work defines you," says Steve Jobs, Pixar's CEO.[82]

> • *Macy's department stores.* Macy's began sending top managers to a class on supervising employees that included lessons on Generation X. "Some of the older management needed to recognize that life has changed," says Lawrence Naishtut, a former vice president of merchant development and recruitment at Macy's East. "Who cares whether GenXers are good or bad? The bottom line is that they are the future."[83]

"Just look at the companies this generation has started, in the Silicon Valley and elsewhere," says Maggie Jackson. "Their offices are freewheeling, egalitarian, fast-paced, colorful kinds of places, where play is taken as seriously as work. It's no wonder that many conservative companies run by aging baby boomers have been having a hard time trying to adapt to this younger crowd."[84] Savvy managers know, though, that the only choice is to adapt.

Talent Scouting

Employee retention is one of the most talked-about and critical issues in American business today. It is now a commonly understood problem—and a major issue and challenge. Not only is the "churn" (turnover) a concern; companies need to also understand how to find and retain top talent, in bull and bear economies alike.

Some companies are beginning to see this, but more than a few are "clue impaired." For example, at Oracle, research shows that it costs close to $70,000 to replace an employee at a mid-level position. So, a churn of four thousand employees a year costs $280 million! That's a lot of money.

Large companies have to deal with employee turnover on a massive scale. On the other hand, they frequently have a great deal more resources than their smaller counterparts. *TrendSmart* leaders in small companies understand that they can indeed compete with larger, older companies. They know that there are many other "carrots" out there today, subtle ones, which enable their firms to tilt the field to their advantage.

The primary advantage of a small company is that it is small. So smaller firms can offer many attractive incentives not feasible at a larger competitor. For example, consider the following:

- The chance to make a difference
- The opportunity to enter at the ground level
- The opportunity to grow career-based skills that will last a lifetime
- The opportunity to learn, grow, and expand skills
- The opportunity to work with a "diagonal slice" of the company

All of these matter, often even more than salary. Typically, money is third or fourth on the magical list of job incentives. The little, special things mean a lot. For example, one company offers monthly house cleaners for single moms, and another gives out Canondale mountain bikes to top sales staff. An architectural firm set up sleep tents for short naps. A mortgage company has a "sick bank"—since sick days do not accrue, employees can pool their days and offer them to friends at work with serious problems (a sick child, for example) or a disabling illness.

Such things show what a company values, and they allow employees choices that transcend financial gain.

Location, Location, Location

Motivating top talent assumes, of course, that you have attracted them to your company in the first place. Bill Breen gives some useful tips from the high-tech sector in an article in *Fast Company* magazine. Breen rightly points out that *where* the job is located can often be as important as *what* the job is. So, when considering where to locate or relocate, today's companies would do well to consider the following high-tech lessons:

1. *Talent seeks out places with real assets.* It's no surprise that techies want a plug-and-play community—one where a new hire moves in, plugs in, and within three weeks has built a network of friends and colleagues.

2. *To become talent magnets, cities must have something for everyone.* The "creative" high-tech folks are flocking to three types of new-economy hot spots: the traditional, high-tech industrial complex; the "latte town," with easily accessible outdoor amenities; and the new urban technology centers.

3. *Talent wants job options.* New-economy workers think of their careers as portfolios of experiences. When they size up a region, the first thing that they look for is a thick labor market—a wide variety of employment opportunities that will sustain a career in the high-tech field.

4. *Talent seeks inclusivity.* A company or a city that really understands how to make itself competitive accepts talented people from all walks of life. True indicators include cities with a significant gay population and companies that offer domestic-partner benefits.

5. *Talent seeks out places that conserve time.* In both their cities and their companies, people want high energy, convenient amenities, and a sense of fun. They also want efficient amenities—ones that are instantaneously available and

diverse enough to attend to needs that might crop up "someday."

6. *Business is not a spectator sport.* Knowledgeable workers don't want to spectate; they want to participate. Cities are building sports stadiums, but talent wants bike paths. They are active people who want fun, music, and open spaces. They'll choose an afternoon of Ultimate Frisbee over one in front of the tube. Cities that understand this leverage their music scene, for example, or their independent-film community to project the image of a unique quality of life for high-tech workers.[85]

Interview Applicants Not on Their Past But on Their Future

Assuming you have found a way to attract talented applicants, what then? What about the hiring process itself? Questionnaires may be of suspect value. But more troubling, interviews are often too focused on the past: "So what was your biggest success? Your biggest challenge?" Things move fast today, and the past is becoming less and less relevant. That's why, says Gina Imperato, some companies have stopped relying on traditional interviews.

"FutureView," says Imperato, "is another approach to hiring, which focuses on what is to come upon hiring. It's the mirror image of an interview, with job simulations over the Internet that let a candidate do some actual work over the Web for the team to see, and a video feed of the team back so that the candidate will see who she would be working with."[86]

TrendSmart Tip: Interview applicants not on the basis of what they've done in the past but on what they can do for you in the future.

Talent Keeping

Some companies have elevated the talent-keeping process to a fine art over many years. Consider the findings from Kepner-Tregoe research on eleven companies renowned for low turnover and high employee loyalty:

1. Retention leaders manage the entire context in which people perform: strategies, systems, policies, decision making, and other practices. They manage people, not just retain people.
2. These companies have a culture of caring, balanced with a tradition of excellence.
3. All have a number of avenues for resolving conflicts.
4. They first take stock, then take action. That is, they know the danger signs of lagging employee loyalty and have measures to deal with it.
5. They keep their eyes on high performers and reward them for performance.
6. They view people management as a strategic business issue. In each company, employees are seen as drivers of financial performance.
7. These companies relentlessly pursue continuous improvement.[87]

Reading between the Lines...of Evaluations

Performance reviews and annual evaluations have become increasingly complex and limited due, in part, to the difficulty of obtaining accurate and useful background information on employees because of labor laws and privacy protections. A little humor makes this point clear. Consider this creative recommendation:

1) Bob Smith, my assistant programmer, can always be found

2) hard at work in his cubicle. Bob works independently, without

3) wasting company time talking to colleagues. Bob never

4) thinks twice about assisting fellow employees, and he always

5) finishes given assignments on time. Often he takes extended

6) measures to complete his work, sometimes skipping coffee

7) breaks. Bob is a dedicated individual who has absolutely no

8) vanity in spite of his high accomplishments and profound

9) knowledge in his field. I firmly believe that Bob can be

10) classed as a high-caliber employee, the type which cannot be

11) dispensed with. Consequently, I duly recommend that Bob be

12) promoted to executive management, and a proposal will be

13) executed as soon as possible.

Addendum: That idiot Bob was standing over my shoulder while I wrote the report. Kindly reread the odd-numbered lines only.

The High Cost of Going Freelance

There are downsides even to those who only have to evaluate and review themselves. Managing your time and keeping your priorities straight, for example, require a great deal of discipline and are difficult to self-evaluate. There are many other downsides to free agency that are far more subtle.

"You have to look long and hard at [free agency], because being a successful free agent takes time," warns Rob Steir, CEO at MBAFreeAgents.com, a job site for M.B.A.s based in New York.[88] I often advise people who are ready to hang out their shingle that starting out on your own is a bit like being pregnant; it takes about nine months before the first check will clear the bank.

In addition, self-employed freelancers need cash on hand to cover living and business expenses in case the well runs dry (three months' worth is recommended). Freelancing is a bad fit for those who need to know when the next paycheck is coming in.

Being a free agent is also less than ideal for people who thrive on daily interaction with others. While some jobs allow contractors to work on site, many require them to work from their own home or office. So if you can't imagine a workday without long talks around the coffee machine, you may find the isolation of freelance life too much to bear.

Global Retirement Issues

The decisions one faces at the beginning of one's free-agent career continue uninterrupted until that point comes when you consider how to wind down a career.

No one works forever, but from nation to nation, some of us work longer than others. Data from *The Economist* is quite striking. In the United States, only half the men aged sixty to sixty-four are still in the labor force. That is more than Germany, where just over one-third still work—or France and the Netherlands, where the figure is less than one-fifth.[89] Retirement, a concept that barely existed a century ago, now begins so early, and people live so much longer, that employees will spend only half their lives in the workforce.

In Japan, according to Mariko Fujiwara, an industrial anthropologist who runs a think-tank for Hakuhodo, the nation's second-largest advertising agency, most companies are bringing down the retirement age from the traditional fifty-seven to fifty or thereabouts—and in some cases, such as Nissan, to forty-five.

In Germany, reports Patrick Pohl, spokesman for Hoechst, "perhaps the main reason for replacing older workers is that it makes it easier to 'defrost' the corporate culture. Older workers are less willing to try a new way of thinking. Younger workers are cheaper and more flexible."

In OECD (Organization for Economic Co-Operation and Development) countries, as Exhibit 14-2 shows, dramatic shifts are occurring in the relationship between life span and length of employment.

Exhibit 14-2. The Changing Relationship Between Life Span and Years of Employment

We are at the beginning of an estimated thirty-year cycle in which workers will retire earlier and live longer. Further complicating the matter, in an increasing number of instances, companies are reluctant to perpetually tie pay increases to longevity. So take away those seniority-based pay scales and look for other incentives to keep the workforce productive and active longer.

In Belgium, faced with the need to cut staff costs, and having decided to concentrate cuts on fifty-five to sixty-year-olds, IBM set up a separate company called SkillTeam, which reemployed any of the early retired who wanted to go on working up to the age of sixty. An employee who joined SkillTeam at the age of fifty-five on a five-year contract would work for 58 percent of his time, over the full period, for 88 percent of his last IBM salary. The company offered services to IBM, thus allowing it to retain access to some of the intellectual capital it would otherwise have lost.

In Britain, a study by David Storey of Warwick University found that 70 percent of businesses started by people over fifty-five survived, compared with an average of only 19 percent across all age groups. There is, then, some level of success that accrues with age. Nonetheless, it is quite likely that in the near future, capitalist economies will create public policy that allows for the pro rata reduction of salaries at certain age levels. Viewed over four

---

decades of employment, income may begin to look like a Gaussian curve, peaking in the middle years of employment.

**TrendSmart Tip: Don't be surprised if your staff
job-hops...just let them know they're welcome to come
back and work for the company at any time in the future.
An "open door" attitude makes good business sense.**

The *TrendSmart* leader understands the changing and evolving
nature of the workforce. With sound information and trend analysis,
planning for future staffing and skill-sets is made infinitely easier.

TrendSmart Tips

- Employees today see themselves as "free agents," because they *want* to work at a particular job, at a particular point in time, for particular personal reasons.
- Engage employees by giving them high-intensity, short-duration project assignments, working in changeable teams.
- Pay employees based on their performance, not their longevity with the company.
- Mentor your employees and allow them to pursue unconventional career paths within the company. There's no such thing as a straight "corporate ladder" anymore.
- Interview applicants not on the basis of what they've done in the past but on what they can do for you in the future.
- Don't be surprised if your staff job-hops...just let them know they're welcome to come back and work for the company at any time in the future. An "open door" attitude makes good business sense.

Chapter 15

Fringe Deficits

Where People Weigh the Benefits and Liabilities of Work, Products, and Services

⊕ ⊕ ⊕

"Companies are like Roach Motels. Good people
go in, and nothing comes out."

—*John Brockman, literary agent*

TrendSmart leaders who understand the working contradictions of today's workplace are well ahead of the game. Many employees choose to work and to work hard not because of the money but, as we have seen, for a variety of other reasons, such as growth and professional development, the chance to make a difference, or the opportunity to work *on* a company as much as *for* it. Obstacles that prevent these are deficits of employment; opportunities that encourage these become benefits of employment—and often they do not cost a penny.

**TrendSmart Tip: Many employees choose to
work hard, not because of the money, but for a
variety of other reasons, such as growth and
professional development, the chance to
make a difference, or the opportunity to
work *on* a company as much as *for* it.**

A company today needs to be mindful not only of its "fringe benefits" but also of what I call its "fringe deficits." Even in tough times, employees know they have some options, and they will compare the ratio of deficits to benefits among each of their employment options. Among the more obvious forms of fringe deficits are the lack of opportunity to advance, archaic policies and procedures, inflexibility, lackluster work styles of tenured or vested employees, and assorted versions of myopic nepotism.

With ready access to data and information, employees today are making increasingly informed decisions about where to work and whether to stay, weighing the pluses and minuses. Often, too, candidates can easily obtain the inside scoop on a company—information formerly available to just a few industry experts.

For a decade or more, there has emerged a great deal of useful information about the benefits and deficits of the workplace.

**TrendSmart Tip: Make sure your company doesn't have
"fringe deficits," obstacles that get in the way of keeping
great employees, such as job inflexibility or the lack of
opportunity for advancement.**

Ferreting Out Fringe Deficits

By their nature, fringe deficits can be subtle and difficult to spot. *TrendSmart* leaders, therefore, adhere to the 1960s mantra of "question everything." They ask questions rather than purport to have all the answers. For example, if you want to track down the fringe deficits in your company, try questioning the following:

- *Fresh eyes.* Ask your newest employee or customer to tell you what has gone "right" and what has gone "wrong" in their dealing with you thus far. Then take their observations seriously.
- *Sacred cows.* Give your processes a reality check, paying special attention to "sacred cows"—policies that have outlived their usefulness. Notice where employees "work around the system" to get things done. These are sure indicators of fringe deficits. Determine whether policy and procedure manuals accurately reflect the way things are. Then rectify outdated rules, needless paperwork, and unnecessary bottlenecks.
- *Departing employees.* Take advantage of the wealth of information available in the exit interview. You can learn valuable lessons from those who are leaving your company for greener pastures. Departing employees can provide vital insights into your company's most insidious fringe deficits—the ones no existing employee may be willing to risk talking about. Then use those insights to make life better for those who remain.

**TrendSmart Tip: Ferret out possible fringe deficits
by asking departing employees what they think
of your company as well as asking new employees.
Also, look closely at any "sacred cows" that
may be making work less easy or fun.**

From Deficit to Benefit: "Give Them What They Want"

TrendSmart leaders today look for ways to GTWTW (Give Them What They Want) says Laurie Masters, free-agent editor at Precision Revision. The leader's job is to offer, even dazzle people with, opportunities for growth, freedom, and building their skills. The challenge is to spot deficits and turn them into benefits, which can often be done with relative ease. Consider the following examples.

Time Off

Dawson Personnel Systems recently tested a non-cash benefit that "ended up outstripping all our expectations," says vice president and partner David DeCapua. "We decided to see what would happen if we offered our employees generous amounts of time off once their jobs were completed," says Dawson. "We got the idea from looking at employee surveys....It seems that the number-one thing employees want more of is not money. Rather, more than anything else, the survey found employees want...to have time off with their families."[90]

Similarly, in 1996, Eddie Bauer, Inc., the giant retailer of casual apparel and home furnishings, introduced "Balance Day." Employees refer to the extra day off a year to do whatever they want as "Call in Well Day." "It's a huge hit," said Sue Storgaard.[91] Her title, director of work/life—rather than work/family—services, also shows Bauer's desire to help all employees (including those without families and its thousands of part-timers) find balance in their lives.

Vacations

Set vacations may be a fringe deficit for many employees. Let's say that you have a young work force, including a high number of young mothers. And say that your vacation policy is designed for employees to take their vacations one week at a time. To a young mother, having ten three-day weekends a year or the ability to take a vacation day at any time to attend a child's ballet class or soccer game may be the best vacation she could have. Change the policy; squelch the deficit!

Job Titles

For many years, job titles had very little relationship to the job itself. Perhaps in response to this, a recent fad (not a trend) in corporate circles has been to provide people with concocted titles such as Chief People Officer, Chief Transformation Officer, or Chief Culture Officer.[92] *Fortune* magazine recently dubbed Chief e-Commerce Officer the "hottest new job title."

At PSS World Medical, truck drivers have business cards listing their title as CEO, presumably because when they are standing in front of the customer, "They are the CEO."[93]

"Everyone can be chief of something in business these days," says Roger Herman of the Herman Group, a North Carolina consulting firm. "A chief in your title will boost your ego and maybe your performance but usually not your compensation."

Job Security

For some workers, at a given point in their lives, job security is deemed the single most important fringe benefit of employment. At NUMMI (New United Motors Manufacturing, Inc.), employees are told that no one will be laid off unless the company's survival is threatened.[94] In so doing, NUMMI reduces the fear factor and increases loyalty and productivity.

Bonuses

In many jobs, particularly sales positions, annual income is often tied to performance bonuses rather than fixed salaries. In some companies, the ability to offer bonuses has been delegated to a much wider array of employees. At Cisco, for example, during prosperous times, anyone could give anyone else an on-the-spot bonus of as much as $5,000 with the boss's approval.[95]

Bill Palmer of Commercial Casework devised a creative way to administer employee bonuses. He put together an employee group of seven volunteers to research and design the company's bonus plan, partially eliminating the human-resources department of his $10 million woodworking and cabinetry shop in Fremont, California. Palmer says that he not only got good information about how to motivate his employees, but he also got more informed employees. "They learned a whole lot more about what it means to give and get a bonus," says Palmer. "They saw how difficult it was and wound up really taking ownership of the process."[96]

Financial Assistance

As the lives of employees change, there are times when access to additional financial resources can dramatically affect employee productivity and/or loyalty. Mindful of this, The Men's Wearhouse clothing stores offer interest-free loans to employees having financial difficulties.[97]

Several American public-school districts have faced high teacher turnover, due, in large part, to high housing costs. In response, these districts offer mortgage subsidy programs to teachers who remain five or more years on the job.

Charitable Giving

Ken Blanchard, author of *The One-Minute Manager*, has even turned philanthropy into a fringe benefit. At the Ken Blanchard company, "We tithe 10 percent of our profit, which last year was $320,000 in donations. We divide it among all of our employees to give away. The lowest-paid employee gets to give $3,000 away and the highest gets to give $3,500. We gave to 160 charities last year. A guy in shipping came up to me with tears in his eyes. He got the chance to give $1,999 to his parish to buy robes for the choir. He's become a local hero."[98]

TrendSmart Tip: Find out what's *really* important to induce employees to stay with your company... whenever possible, give them what they want!

Policy Reform

In nearly every company, there are those chronic drains on employee morale, the subtle or obvious "sacred cows." Mitel Corporation (see chapter 5 for more on Mitel), embarked upon what they refer to as a "sacred cow hunt," much to the delight of employees and management alike. Consider these two examples:

- Prior to Mitel's cow hunt, so many signatures were needed to approve a business trip that Mitel's research and development people rarely visited customers to discuss their needs.
- Mitel engineers responsible for spending hundreds of thousands of dollars had to sign numerous forms before they could even take home a laptop.

Eliminating these needless bottlenecks throughout Mitel dramatically improved that company's productivity and, by extension, the satisfaction of its employees.

A truly savvy manager anticipates not only the fringe deficits that affect employees but also those that affect customers and suppliers, as well—and looks for ways to turn even *those* into benefits. For example, soft-drink manufacturers like Coca-Cola and Pepsi realized that a fringe deficit for most grocery stores was the lack of good inventory controls and systems. At certain account volume levels, the suppliers offered to work with stores on inventory controls in exchange for a more lucrative and/or exclusive contract or in some instances more prominent shelf space.

Benefits Are in the Eye of the Beholder

One challenge companies encounter in their efforts to minimize workplace deficits and maximize benefits is the gap in perception of desired benefits identified by employees versus what their supervisors perceived. In a recent university survey of "what employees want in their jobs," employees and supervisors were asked to rank their preferences.[99] The differences, shown in Exhibit 15-1, were striking.

Exhibit 15-1. Employee Benefits: Employee Perception Versus Supervisor Perception		
	EMPLOYEES	SUPERVISORS
Interesting work	1	5
Appreciation	2	8
Feeling "in" on things	3	10
Job security	4	2
Good pay	5	1
Promotions	6	3
Good working conditions	7	4
Personal growth	8	7
Help/personal problems	9	9
Tactful discipline	10	6

Clearly, there is a gap in perception. Supervisors try to motivate employees with higher pay, greater job security, and frequent promotions. On the other hand, employees want to do interesting work, be appreciated for that work, and feel included in decisions. It's no wonder that problems often arise when even well-intentioned supervisors assume they know the desires of those who report to them. Savvy supervisors are aware of actual desires and seek to find rewards and incentives that match the employees' needs.

Nine Actions to Make Employees Feel Valued

Given the disparity between what employees want and what their managers think they want, companies can use all the help they can get in zeroing in on those practices that will really make a difference. To this end, Phillip Britt offers the following tips:

- Talk to employees about their workplace needs, expectations, and suggestions for improvement.
- Develop a profit-sharing or incentive-compensation plan. Consider offering a variety of benefit choices.
- Encourage employees to "own" their work areas, arrange desks and chairs however they like, and surround themselves with pictures, clippings, and other visual images they enjoy.
- Offer flexible work arrangements (compressed schedules, flextime, telecommuting, part-time, job sharing, or sabbaticals).
- Employees who take work home may sometimes bring home into work. Support child care, elder care, and other family needs.
- Create teams focused on well-defined goals with concrete

deadlines, and clarify each member's role.

- Delegate 100 percent of responsibility to employees for something and give them room for creative expression.
- Hire a genuinely diverse pool of employees and reflect diversity in the leadership of your organization.
- Tie rewards, promotions, compensation, and increases in responsibility and authority directly to performance.[100]

New-Age Currency

Management expert R. Brayton Bowen, who penned a bestselling book titled *Recognizing and Rewarding Employees*, recommends a "whole-person approach" for employee compensation. He suggests that "new-age currency"—intangibles like meaningful work and managerial respect—not just dollars, appeal to today's workforce. "Work designed to be intrinsically meaningful and extrinsically rewarding is what propels most workers, even in basic jobs like maintenance," says Bowen. The challenge is to tie basic work—or complex challenges—to the larger mission and purpose of the company. "It's key to compensating people in today's harsh workplace of low commitment and high anxiety," Bowen explains.

Bowen says that too many working people today are being denied even basic respect. "More than half of the managers I've interviewed admit they give no recognition at all."[101] Although back-patting won't yield a motivated workforce, it is one tool that a successful manager uses generously.

Garnering the Benefits of Teams

Sometimes what seems to be a benefit, if improperly implemented, can become a deficit. For example, most companies are highly committed to the idea of "team building" and "natural work teams." Too often, however, working as a team looks much better on the organizational chart than in reality. What makes a successful team? How can teamwork become a fringe benefit? In *High Five! The Magic of Working Together,* Ken Blanchard and coauthors Sheldon Bowles, Don Carew, and Eunice Parisi-Carew write about fictional youth hockey players who learn the lessons of teamwork through the acronym PUCK:

- **P**rovide a clear purpose and shared values and goals.
- **U**nleash and develop skills.
- **C**reate team power.
- **K**eep the accent on the positive through repeated recognition and reward.

Positive feedback "is the breakfast of champions," Blanchard said, while posing the rhetorical question, "How many of you are sick and tired of all the praise and compliments you've been getting?" No hands were raised.[102]

Developing a sense of team spirit is a crucial part of making good teamwork a reality. Some common pitfalls to team-based success include:

- *Not taking time in the beginning.* People never understand why the team was created, what their role is within the team, and what the team's role is within the organization.
- *Believing everything has to be done as a team effort.* Sometimes people should work on a project alone or in pairs, because involving the entire team would slow things down.

- *Not enough side-by-side accountability.* Team members have to be accountable to one another, not just to the boss.
- *Not having enough needed resources, especially time.*
- *Leaders who won't let go.* Or sometimes the followers are to blame because they won't take over the leadership role on a particular project, even though they might have the most expertise in that area.
- *Not focusing enough on excellence and creativity.* Sometimes team members are so involved with relationships that they overlook important aspects of the project.
- *Inadequate planning.*
- *Not enough management support.*
- *The inability to deal with conflict.* If there is too much emphasis on team harmony, people won't challenge ideas, even when they should.
- *Not enough training at all levels on group skills.*

Workplace Fun

A large body of research on team productivity consistently identifies a strong correlation between productivity and pleasure. When "work" is "fun," high performance commonly follows. Three out of four Americans are dissatisfied with or fundamentally disconnected from their jobs, according to a recent *Gallup Management Journal* survey. "Granted, workers have been miserable for centuries," says Matthew Boyle, "but now that the dot-com boom, which spawned a host of worker-friendly initiatives, has ended, is the joy gone for good?" The simple answer is no.

In an effort to keep employees engaged, even traditional companies have implemented a host of lighthearted activities in recent years. Exhibit 15-2 lists a few.

**Exhibit 15-2. How Some Companies
Foster Workplace Fun**

- *Capital One.* A "fun budget" of $80 per employee per quarter to spend on activities such as white-water rafting.
- *CDW Computer Centers.* Krispy Kreme doughnuts once a month and free Dairy Queen every summer Wednesday. If the company meets sales goals, CDW offers an "old-timer" benefit for anyone with three years' service: a free trip for you and your family anywhere in the continental U.S. (awarded every other year).
- *Southwest Airlines.* Spirit parties, gate- and cake-decorating contests, barbecues, and chili cook-offs are just some of the events planned by local "culture committees."
- *Snapple.* Theme Fridays during the summer (tie-dye day, silly hat day). One year the company built a makeshift miniature golf course inside its corporate headquarters, with each department constructing a hole from materials they use during the course of the day.[103]

Satire and Sarcasm: Workplace Barometers

Unfortunately, sometimes the only kind of fun evident amongst a company's workers are the cynical jabs, disguised as humor, that circulate from computer to computer, cubicle to cubicle. One of my litmus tests of the health of a company's "culture" is the extent to which its employees identify with these bits of comic relief. *TrendSmart* leaders pay careful attention to this phenomenon. Often, it is a direct road map to the core issues that affect morale, productivity, and profitability. Exhibit 15-3 is intended to be humorous, but pay close attention to the content behind the chuckles.

Exhibit 15-3. You Know You Work in Corporate America If...

- You've sat at the same desk for four years and worked for three different companies.
- Your company welcome sign is attached with Velcro.
- Your résumé is on a diskette in your pocket.
- You learn about your layoff on CNN.
- Your supervisor doesn't have the ability to do your job.
- Salaries of executive board members are higher than all the Third World countries' annual budgets combined.
- You think lunch is just a meeting to which you drive.
- It's dark when you drive to and from work.
- Weekends are those days your spouse makes you stay home.
- Art involves a white board.
- You're already late on the assignment you just got.
- Your boss's favorite lines are "when you get a few minutes," "in your spare time," "when you're freed up," and "I have an opportunity for you."
- The only reason you recognize your kids is because their pictures are hanging in your cube.
- You only know how you look under fluorescent lighting.

Suckcess and Despair: Capitalizing on Fringe Deficits

Great cynics apparently think alike. For example, Suckcess, Inc. and Despair, Inc. have created retail product lines that capitalize on the prevalence of fringe deficits in the corporate world. These small companies have launched lines of cards, T-shirts, and other items that look a lot like the usual pap but are gleefully designed to ruin your day.[104] Despair's products are bought mostly from their website (www.despair.com). Suckcess cards are sold in stores by Recycled Paper Products, as well as at Suckcess's site (www.hellisstillhell.com).

TrendSmart Tip: Pay attention to workplace humor, whether it's jokes at the company's expense or sarcasm and irony.

Both lines feature images and headlines that appear to be of the usual "successories" type; then they zap the reader with an unexpected, cynical, and/or sarcastic sentiment, such as "NEVER QUIT: Wait to be fired. You get more." Or "FAILURE: When your best just isn't good enough."

Upping the Ante on Satire—120 Percent

Near Bridge, Inc. trends editor Steve Weiss sent me the spoof press release shown in Exhibit 15-4, which targets the fringe deficits of a high-tech company. Since I believe the content to be broadly applicable, and I believe, too, in the power of sarcasm, the names have been changed to protect the not-so-innocent objects of tongue-in-cheek ridicule.

Exhibit 15-4. Layoffs with a Sense of Humor

Northern, Calif.—Big Old Company (BOC) announced today that it will reduce its current workforce by an unprecedented 120 percent by the end of the fiscal year, believed to be the first time a major corporation has laid off more employees than it actually has.

BOC stock soared more than 12 points on the news.

The reduction decision, announced Thursday, came after a year-long internal review of cost-cutting procedures, said BOC CEO Ben Fitte. The initial report concluded the company would save $1.2 billion by eliminating 20 percent of its 108,000 employees.

From there, said Fitte, "it didn't take a genius to figure out that if we cut 40 percent of our workforce, we'd save $2.4 billion, and

---

if we cut 100 percent of our workforce, we'd save $6 billion. But then we thought, why stop there? Let's cut another 20 percent and save $7 billion.

"We believe in increasing shareholder value, and we believe that by decreasing expenditures, we enhance our competitive cost position and our bottom line," he added.

BOC plans to achieve the 100 percent internal reduction through layoffs, attrition, and early retirement packages. To achieve the 20 percent in external reductions, the company plans to involuntarily downsize twenty-two thousand non-BOC employees who presently work for other companies.

"We pretty much picked them out of a hat," said Fitte.

Among firms BOC has picked as "External Reduction Targets," or ERTs, are Quaker Oats; AMR Corporation, parent of American Airlines; Callaway Golf; and Charles Schwab and Co. BOC's plan presents a "win-win" for the company and ERTs, said Fitte, as any savings by ERTs would be passed on to BOC, while the ERTs themselves would benefit by the increase in stock price that usually accompanies personnel cutback announcements.

"We're also hoping that since, over the years, we've been really helpful to a lot of companies, they'll do this for us kind of as a favor," said Fitte.

Legally, pink slips sent out by BOC would have no standing at ERTs unless those companies agreed. While executives at ERTs declined to comment, employees at those companies said they were not inclined to cooperate.

"This is ridiculous. I don't work for BOC. They can't fire me," said Chris Brown, a twenty-year employee at one company.

Reactions like that, replied Fitte, "are not very sporting."

"It's a little early to tell, but by eliminating all its employees,

BOC may jeopardize its market position and could, at least theoretically, cease to exist," said Catcher.

Fitte, however, urged patience: "To my knowledge, this hasn't been done before, so let's just wait and see what happens."

Why People Stay

Certainly, humor has its place. It makes time pass quickly, it makes the workday more pleasant, and it can enhance our performance. When humor is an important part of a company culture, that company typically experiences higher employee loyalty. There is much more to be said, though, about ways to overcome the obstacles—the fringe deficits—that push people out of one place and on to another. Employees appreciate not being micromanaged and having a clear set of expectations and goals.

What do you do if your employee comes to you and says, "I've got this great offer...what are you going to do to keep me?" There are several factors to consider here. Realistically, just how valuable is that employee? What are the accurate replacement costs? What are the repercussions of making a "deal" with one employee in the eyes of others? Many times it is clearly best to make a deal and keep the employee there...and happy.

Finally, bear in mind that some employees are not meant to be keepers. What used to be a forty-year "career job" is now a four-year cycle at best. On average, people change jobs every four years, and careers every eight to ten years. This is neither good nor bad...it simply *is*.

TrendSmart Tips

- Many employees choose to work hard, not because of the money, but for a variety of other reasons, such as growth and professional development, the chance to make a difference, or the opportunity to work *on* a company as much as *for* it.
- Make sure your company doesn't have "fringe deficits," obstacles that get in the way of keeping great employees, such as job inflexibility or the lack of opportunity for advancement.
- Ferret out possible fringe deficits by asking departing employees what they think of your company as well as asking new employees. Also, look closely at any "sacred cows" that may be making work less easy or fun.
- Find out what's *really* important to induce employees to stay with your company...whenever possible, give them what they want!
- Pay attention to workplace humor, whether it's jokes at the company's expense or sarcasm and irony.

Chapter 16

Perpetual Innovation

Where Innovation Is Everybody's Everyday Job

⊕ ⊕ ⊕

"No ideas but in things."
—*William Carlos Williams, poet*

These days, the conventional wisdom of "plan your work and work your plan" has been significantly modified. *TrendSmart* leaders know that innovation is the better part of valor, and they adhere to a new ironic maxim, "plan on changing your plans." Innovation is the ability to take a creative idea and implement it. In companies that are repeatedly successful, innovation has been built into their corporate cultures through astute hiring and incentive practices. In these companies, innovation is encouraged and rewarded for each and every employee. In that sense, innovation is everybody's everyday job.

The adage that "the only constant is change" is still true, yet it is rarely factored into the planning process. Worse still, many companies believe that they have managed the status quo, and so they assume, understandably, that they can manage change. In my experience, it is quite the contrary. Texans have it right when they say, "Managing change is a lot like trying to nail Jell-O to a tree!"

Unfortunately, past success is too often a deterrent to future success. Certainly one reason for this is that success often breeds complacency. When you are on a roll, when everything is going right, it is very difficult to discipline yourself to veer from the norm and keep new ideas coming through the pipeline.

You Ain't Nuttin' But a Hound Dog!

Pat Lynch recently told a story that speaks to just how difficult it can be to innovate.

A man went to visit his friend, and this old hound dog was lying on the porch. Every once in a while this hound dog would let out an awful howl as if he were in pain, but he made no movement.

After a couple times the man asked, "What's wrong with your dog? Is he sick or dying?" The friend told him the hound dog was lying on a nail that was sticking out from the wooden porch, and it hurt the dog. Thus the reason for the awful howls.

The visitor was horrified, and asked his friend how he could let the old dog suffer like that, and just sit there and do nothing. The friend told the man, "He will move when it hurts bad enough."

In business today, so many things hurt so badly that an encouraging call to action has surfaced in the battlefields of commerce. *TrendSmart* managers won't accept the attitude—or the employee— who will innovate only if it's painful to do so. Today, even that poor old hound dog would be well advised to "git a move on." As an Oracle Consulting ad says, "Don't just think outside the box. Live outside the box."

A company that is change-enabled and innovation-friendly has a distinct competitive advantage. After all, you can quickly create a product or service; you can quickly develop a brand these days; you can even very quickly gain market share—for a while. But, it takes *time* to build a culture that is innovative and sees change as its partner. And, once achieved, therein lies the competitive advantage.

TrendSmart Tip: Build innovation into your corporate culture from the get-go: hire innovative employees and make sure that innovation is an institutionalized practice.

Even though many kinds of change are quite literally beyond our control, by institutionalizing innovation, we can partner with change. Change is not done merely for its own sake; change is planned into the culture, the strategy, and the systems of the company—and for good reason. As Alfred Edward Perlman advises, "After you've done a thing the same way for two years, look it over carefully. After five years, look at it with suspicion. After ten years, throw it out and start over."[105]

My mother used to tell me that she always worked hard and had a passion for life because, she realized, "nothing in nature retires." There is no chaise lounge for an aging wolf. There are no hammocks for butterflies. There are no naps for the ocean. And so not to constantly change is, literally, unnatural.

Staving Off Myopia

Institutionalized innovation offers a road map that guides and directs change. Today, if you are not being innovative, you can hit the small, myopic targets and still miss winning the grand prizes. In this business environment, the innovator is one who can maximize responsiveness to the marketplace and work on many levels simultaneously.

Where innovation is institutionalized, the ability to get from point A to point B is encouraged and allows considerable leeway to find the most direct route for the conditions at hand. It is as though in such an environment there exists an organization equivalent of a global positioning system, or GPS.

There is one catch; in today's competitive world, we no longer have the simple route with only two stops, points A and B. Factor in points C (for customer), M (for markets), V (for value proposition), and P (for profitability), and the organizational GPS is given a real challenge. Because of the complexity of the business terrain, institutionalized innovation—where the pursuit of innovation is done collegially—is an invaluable asset to any organization.

TrendSmart Tip: Don't wait for a situation to become painful before changing it; innovation should be a constant goal.

Knowing which routes lead to innovation is one of the gifts of a business leader. *TrendSmart* leaders today treat their employees as a good director treats an artist. "I always use some kind of a jazz mentality when I'm dealing with the artist," says Pavel Brun, artistic director of Cirque du Soleil. "I don't need to write every single note for them as long as I know that they can play. I am giving them direction…[but] the rhythm they use is entirely up to them. They know that they have to go from here to there. How is a question of their creativity."[106]

Continuous Hiring

In successful companies, institutionalized innovation begins with attracting the right people, at the right time, for the right jobs. "Traditionally," says John Sullivan, head of the human-resource management program at San Francisco State University, "companies get serious about hiring when they have a specific opening....I call that approach coincidence hiring." In contrast to coincidence hiring, Sullivan proposes *continuous* hiring. Companies "don't want to hire unemployed people or unhappy people. They want to hire people who can make a difference, the best of the best," says Sullivan. "You have to go from coincidence hiring to continuous hiring."[107]

As Gina Imperato has pointed out, "One of the best ways to create a pipeline of talented future employees is to identify the best and the brightest people in your geographical area—whether or not they work in your company today—and then to stay in touch with them. You may have go to the right conferences, hang out in chat rooms on the Net, or gain access to the right online mailing lists. So be it." You have to create what Sullivan calls "learning networks" that help you meet great people—the kind of people you want working for your company—even if those people aren't looking for a job right now.

TrendSmart Tip: Create a pipeline of talented future employees so you're never caught empty-handed.

According to Imperato, among the techniques learned by those companies who use a continuous hiring program are:

- Assume that talented people who decide to leave their jobs will be on the market for one day.
- Prequalify people for jobs. Some companies go so far as to give out coupons that say, in effect, "You're hired, say when." Of course, such "ninja hiring" practices take organizational confidence—confidence in both the corporate culture as well as in the economy.
- Don't subject great people to empty formalities. Savvy, talented people are not dummies. And like your best customers,

they need to feel that they are special. If you are hiring them in part for their creative and flexible natures, it is counterproductive to subject them to rigid and formalized hiring barriers. An empty process full of busywork sends a clear message to the prospect: beware.

"In the search for the very best, Help Wanted ads may be more counterproductive than productive in the sense that they basically announce that you don't know where to find the sort of people you're looking for," says Imperato. "To stay on top of knowing where the talented people are, one of the first things you should do when you hire a new employee is to ask him or her, 'Who are five others whom you know? How can we persuade them to join us? How can you help us strike up relationships with them?'"

Not only does the networking process of "entrance interviews" provide an ongoing database of talent, it also makes good fiscal sense. One of the least documented costs to a company is for the finding and hiring of new talent. At Cisco, 50 to 60 percent of hires come from employee referrals. They have even gone so far as to create a program, "Make Friends @ Cisco," that matches Cisco employees with people who have expressed an interest in coming to work at Cisco at some later date. It's designed to create a learning relationship.

TrendSmart Tip: Use unusual and innovative hiring practices to attract innovative employees.

"It's easier to be a great manager—and a great company—if you hire well,"[108] says Michael McNeal, director of corporate employment at Cisco Systems, Inc. Hiring well means thinking well about recruiting strategies, because even in tough times, companies want the best and the brightest. And, in fact, in tough times the talent pool is deeper.

Having institutionalized innovation in the hiring process, and knowing full well that great talent was available, McNeal's team put up the first Cisco information booth at the local home and garden show. What do programmers and roses have in common? Demographics. Given the high price of real estate in northern California, McNeal figured that anyone who could afford a home, let alone a garden, had to be at the top of their professional game. He was right. The talent harvest from the home and garden show exceeded even his expectations.

Perhaps more important, he could prove it. Innovative thinking often works best when you track the results of an initiative. "If a manager desperately needs people," says McNeal, "and I walk in and say, 'Let's spend the $30,000 on the Santa Clara Wine and Arts Festival instead of a newspaper ad'—that's not an easy conversation to have. So it's important to build systems that track results. Otherwise, you won't be able to shift mind-sets. And you won't get the support you need." Measuring the outcomes of innovation is an indication that innovation has become institutionalized.

Once, by any number of innovative means, you have managed to hire the best and the brightest, the next challenge begins: how to grow and nurture the new, or young, worker. In the section that follows, we examine this further.

Managing a Younger Workforce

We're all familiar with the term "downsizing," coined in the early 1990s to describe how companies reduced the number of employees to reduce costs—sometimes employees who had worked there ten, twenty, and even thirty years. Downsizing brought short-term profitability, but in the long haul, it undermined productivity and the whole idea of corporate loyalty.

There are challenges of managing a younger workforce today, so many in fact that I coined a new word for one of these. With the crash of many dot-coms has come "dot-sizing"! Dot-sizing refers to all those who got "pink slips" and are using their stock options as kindling to light the fire in their overpriced fireplace.

So, now we have the broader workforce, from ages twenty to sixty-five, *all* of whom are disillusioned a bit, all of whom are wary, all of whom are looking at their futures more soberly in the wake of adversity in the workplace. If you add downsizing and dot-sizing together, you get a new perspective on how the managing of the younger workforce is evolving. Employees of all ages are looking at their lives, bosses, and benefits differently.

TrendSmart Tip: Mentor the young workforce in order to build an innovative company.

Employees today are motivated differently. You can no longer get a sixty-hour workweek from a younger worker just by holding out "stock options" or the "carrot" of instant wealth. They've been there, done that, and *lost* their T-shirt!

The newer benefits at innovative companies, assembled by *Trend-Smart* managers, have a lot to do with a workforce that is growing up, regardless of age. So, for example, to manage a younger worker today may mean offering benefits such as education/tuition and skill building, ways to season and nurture a good person who happens to be young.

Young workers today have little patience. But I see an increased tolerance, even desire, of multiple age groups to learn from each other. In work as elsewhere, the generations need each other. It's actually very exciting, and very humane too, to watch the emerging cooperative projects that consist of an intergenerational team.

We are not talking chronological age only. There are wise twenty-five-year-olds and silly fifty-five-year-olds. Some industries have a young workforce, while other industries have more age diversity. The challenge faced by every *TrendSmart* manager is to find and keep good people and put them in situations where they can thrive, regardless of their age. Maximizing productivity in an international workforce is one of the specialties of my company, Near Bridge.

A good manager is a good teacher and role model. A *TrendSmart* leader has a good heart and good intuition, as well. Like it or not, young workers have grown up in a latchkey world where they take care of each other. They are children of divorced and/or dual-income families, often raised by Nanny Nintendo and the family dog. So mentors and role models are an important and viable strategy if the overall intent is to create an innovative work force in an innovative work environment.

TrendSmart **Tips**

- Build innovation into your corporate culture from the get-go: hire innovative employees and make sure that innovation is an institutionalized practice.
- Don't wait for a situation to become painful before changing it; innovation should be a constant goal.
- Create a pipeline of talented future employees so you're never caught empty-handed.
- Use unusual and innovative hiring practices to attract innovative employees.
- Mentor the young workforce in order to build an innovative company.

Chapter 17

Positive Negatives
Where Building on Strengths Is Not a Weakness

⊕ ⊕ ⊕

"I'd rather have spirited horses than lazy bulls."
—*Moshe Dayan*

The English poet John Keats coined the phrase "negative capability" in a letter he wrote nearly two hundred years ago: "at once it struck me what quality went to form a Man of Achievement, especially in Literature, and which Shakespeare possessed so enormously—I mean Negative Capability, that is, when a man is capable of being in uncertainties, mysteries, doubts, without any irritable reaching after fact or reason."

Today's *TrendSmart* leaders have an intellectual toggle switch—one that enables them to engage and disengage either side of their brain at will. We all have a right and a left brain. The left is the logical, reasoned mind; the right is the intuitive and artistic mind. Most of us, when in positions of fear and/or doubt, to paraphrase Keats, will immediately put our left brains on full tilt. However, today, many situations will require us to use the right side of our brains with regularity.

With Keats's definition as a catalyst, and extending it into a business environment, I found myself focusing on several additional, interrelated topics:

- Build on your strengths.
- Focus on what you do best.
- Turn negatives into positives.

Perhaps a short parable, sent to me by my friend, renowned speaker Pat Lynch, will add to your understanding.

Exhibit 17-1. The Parable of "The Mule in the Well"

"They tell the story of a farmer who owned an old mule who fell, for some strange reason, into the farmer's well.

Fortunately, the water wasn't very deep, so the mule stood on the bottom, and the farmer heard him praying...or whatever mules do when they fall into wells.

After carefully assessing the situation, the farmer felt bad for the old mule...but decided neither the mule nor the well was worth the trouble it'd take to save them. So he called his neighbors together, told them what had happened, and got them to help him haul dirt to bury the old mule in the well and put him out of his misery.

Well, when the dirt started falling the old mule got hysterical. But as the farmer and his neighbors kept shoveling, and the dirt kept falling, the mule got a strange idea: why not just shake off the dirt every time a shovel load hit him...and step up.

And that's what he did, as blow after blow of dirt hit him on the back.

"Shake it off and step up…shake it off and step up…shake it off and step up," the mule kept thinking, over and over, to encourage himself.

And it wasn't long before the old mule, battered and exhausted, stepped up triumphantly over the wall of the well to freedom.

What looked like it was going to bury him had actually helped him, all because of how he *chose* to handle the dirt—the adversity—that others kept shoveling into his life.

"Ever feel like you've got people standing in line to shovel dirt on you?" asks Lynch. "Don't panic, or get bitter, or waste your time and energy feeling sorry for yourself. Just think about the old mule and remember: all that 'dirt' they're giving you…that's supposed to bury you…*always* contains the opportunity you've been waiting for…if you're willing to think different…and step up to more freedom."

Disabling Your Disability

The mule certainly had the right idea. Many people with disabilities have learned the same lesson and found ways to make challenging situations work to their advantage. My dear friend Dr. Carolyn Brown, a pioneer in working with children with neurological disorders, has spent more than thirty years rescuing children and sending them on their way as viable citizens.

Dr. Brown says, "It's a question of knowing how to manage your problems." For example, it's not out of the question for a kid with a learning disability in math to become an engineer. "It won't be true for everybody, but that is possible. There are people with serious disabilities who have become very successful in the business world, and they have three secretaries, one to read for them, one to write for them, somebody else to answer the phone," says Brown.[109]

Be Yourself

TrendSmart managers know that identifying an employee's strengths and then developing them is far more rewarding for the worker and for the organization than constantly shoring up weaknesses. At best, improving weak areas saps time and energy. More often than not, it's an exercise in futility. People gain confidence when you build on their strengths. They take ownership of what they do because they know how to contribute using their natural talents.

TrendSmart Tip: Know your own strengths as well as those of your employees.

Bruce M. Hubby, chairman and founder of PDP, Inc., in Woodland Park, Colorado, observes, "People are at their most productive when they're in a position that lets them draw on their natural strengths and that allows them to be themselves." When people feel the need to act unnaturally, they experience stress, which lowers productivity and leads to job dissatisfaction. So Hubby's company seeks to identify the "basic natural self" of every employee—how they would be if there were no outside pressures. "You need to look for their most intense trait and to create a work environment that capitalizes on it," he adds.[110] Contrary to conventional wisdom, you don't need to know a lot about people's weaknesses either. But you need to know a great deal about their strengths.

This does not mean that leaders won't push people beyond their limits at times. What it does mean is that they place challenges in front of people that play to their strengths, not their weaknesses; their abilities, not their inabilities. In the context of sports and the human body, this seems obvious. A soccer coach would not put her slowest player in the goalie position, a baseball manager would not put a pitcher to bat in the fourth position, and a basketball coach would not expect his shortest player to lead the team in rebounds.

Leaders sometimes intuitively know a person's strengths even when they do not seem obvious to that person. The strengths identified don't have to be long-used talents that the employee is comfortable with and confident about. One great joy of leading comes at those moments when you place someone in a situation they are unsure they can handle and watch them rise to the occasion, bringing untapped skills to solve a problem.

Encourage and Motivate

Encouraging and motivating people are excellent ways to focus on skills, aptitudes, and creativity. Good management today requires instilling the confidence in every employee that their abilities are valued:

- During a training class for Red Robin restaurant employees, Reuben Solis discovered that one of the Hispanic students spoke English as a second language and was having difficulty understanding the materials. Going the extra mile, that night at home Reuben wrote out the key points and activity outlines in Spanish, and thus ensured the team member's participation.[111]
- Jerry Strahan is the general manager for Lucky Dogs, Inc., a $3 million hot-dog-vending company that employs "drifters, alcoholics, petty thieves, not-so-petty thieves, brawlers, and the occasional psychopath." To make Lucky Dogs a profitable enterprise from these "loosest of loose threads," he has learned to be endlessly patient, flexible, and content to take his victories where he finds them.[112]
- A new employee at Gnossos Software speaks of the company president, Steve Kantor: "Steve's a really good teacher....

When I make mistakes, he's not the type to harp on it. He points it out to me and we move on from there."[113]

TrendSmart Tip: Instill confidence in all employees; make sure they know their abilities are valued.

How to Manage Like Joe

Business books often rely on metaphors drawn from sports to make key learning points. I am selective in my own use of such links, as both gender and generational differences limit the ability of the sports theme to carry a universal message. This said, occasionally a sports story does lend itself to a business setting. In a recent issue of *Fortune* magazine, Jerry Useem analyzes the management principles of New York Yankee baseball manager Joe Torre.

Exhibit 17-2. Management Tips from a Great Coach: Joe Torre, Manager of the New York Yankees

- *Ditch the motivational speeches.* Torre relies on frequent one-on-ones, which he uses to both monitor and regulate the psyches of individual players.
- *Be intense, but not tense.* Excess pressure keeps people from playing up to their natural ability, just as it saps creativity and confidence in the workplace.
- *Every employee must feel useful.* Even substitute players can make significant contributions. So Torre always reminds them of their role and importance.
- *Don't punish failure.* Torre stays loyal to slumping players, creating a kind of paradox: a high-performance workplace where failure is tolerated.
- *Manage against the cycle.* When a situation turns

> tense, Torre grows outwardly calmer; when things are
> going well, he turns up the heat.
>
> • *Managing your employees means managing your*
> *boss.* Torre bears the brunt of owner George Stein-
> brenner's impatience, providing a buffer for his
> players.[114]

A good coach, like a good manager, has to know the combination of strengths of each player, as well as how those strengths may blend with those of teammates. "I think you have to look at what your team's strengths are," said Duke University basketball coach Mike Krzyzewski. "In a moment of weakness, or adversity, you tend to think of your weaknesses more than your strengths."[115] In the case of Joe Torre and Mike Krzyzewski, their championship records show us that they are adept at building teams around the strengths of their players, rather than covering up their weaknesses.

TrendSmart managers go to great lengths not only to identify strengths but also to avoid obscuring weaknesses. For example, at dollarDEX, rather than hiding customer complaints from customers or employees, the company displays them on its website, along with explanations or apologies. This has become a highly trafficked part of the dollarDEX site.[116] The lesson learned here is that even a historical weakness can be the foundation of a future success.

Aligning Employees' Skills with Job Descriptions

There are times when a *TrendSmart* manager becomes aware of the lack of alignment between a person's skills and job description. Let's say that you are highly skilled in negotiation, listening, and verbal skills. And let's say that your current position uses few of these skills and is being phased out. Taking the proactive mode, a good manager will look closely at these strengths and see the makings of a good salesperson. You may never have sold a thing, but knowing your manager has confidence in you, you proactively put in your application.

TrendSmart Tip: Align your employees' skills with the right jobs; make sure they're doing a job they're well suited for.

Companies are often aware of the value of aligning certain skills with specific jobs. Consequently, when these companies recruit, they sometimes develop a "profile" of ideal employee characteristics that they deem necessary to remain competitive. These skills vary tremendously and often reflect the values and beliefs of top management.

- At Oracle, if a job seeker has a Type-A, take-no-prisoners attitude, he or she is more likely to be hired than someone with more technical skills but significantly less drive and energy. The job skills, it is assumed, can be taught more readily than the personality traits.

- At Southwest Airlines, humor and hospitality have long been key success indicators in the hiring process. Consequently, applicants who are fun to be around and who care about people are more likely to be hired than other job seekers who have no people skills. A bit of a clownlike attitude goes a long way at Southwest Airlines.

- When Cirque du Soleil hires an athlete, it looks for someone with an artist inside. "Say we have an athlete who can do a triple somersault," says Pavel Brun, artistic director. "My question is, 'How can you express yourself through those triple somersaults?' Sometimes I have very high-profile sportsmen who really do not offer us anything special…. That's a constant question we are asking: 'Tell us who you are.' And that's the search for an artist."[117]

Training: the Strategic Imperative

"The unfortunate mathematical fact," write Charles O'Reilly III and Jeffrey Pfeffer, authors of *Hidden Value*, "is that only 10 percent of the people are going to be in the top 10 percent."[118] But these days successful companies have figured out how to get the best out of *all* of their people, every day. This is where training becomes a vital part of overall business strategy.

"Training isn't just a nice thing to do anymore," says Laurie Bassi, vice president of research at the American Society for Training and Development in Alexandria, Virginia. "Companies are now thinking of training as a strategic imperative."[119] Employees, too, are now well aware that training is essential to their future marketability and are making employment choices based on opportunities for quality training.

TrendSmart Tip: Encourage employee training; it's essential to your employees' success within your company as well as to their own future marketability: a true win/win situation!

Larger companies with in-house training "universities" report several benefits beyond the obvious ones of skill improvement, including the following:

- *Improved recruitment.* Training can be a key recruitment tool. "We're finding that compensation is less of an issue for employees and that growth and career development are more important," says Edward Beaumont, CEO of CoreTech Consulting Group, Inc., in King of Prussia, Pennsylvania. "Most consulting firms have something like this in place."
- *Increased revenues.* Bob Kirkpatrick, CoreTech's CPO— chief people officer (yes, that's his real title)—estimates that the company spends approximately $4,500 per

employee each year on training but says that it's ultimately money well spent.

- *Reduced turnover.* Since Douglas Palley started Unitel University two years ago, average monthly turnover has dropped from 12% to 6%—a dramatic change for a company staffed primarily by low-wage employees.

- *Better employee advancement.* If Unitel employees pass Unitel University freshman courses, they receive a raise of up to 8 percent of their pay. When they successfully complete each level (sophomore, etc.), they earn another raise of up to 8 percent. Over four years, that is a substantial increase, and presumably quite a practical education.

- *A wider talent pool.* "The hiring landscape was pitiful," recalls Jane Callanan, vice president of human resources at i-Cube, a Cambridge, Massachusetts, information-technology consulting-services company. "We wanted to tap into college recruiting, to hire people who were very bright but didn't have several years of work experience." A five-week, nine-to-five program called i-Altitude, staffed primarily by senior managers, allowed the company to hire workers with little experience and then give them the technical training they needed to serve clients. "It really opened the labor market for us," says Callanan. "We can hire a physics major with a 3.8 [grade point average] but with no computer-science training. After five weeks, the person is ready for a project. You can't do that without a good educational program."

Cisco Finds the "Win-Win-Win-Win" Solution

TrendSmart leaders know that things are not always easy on what seemed to be Easy Street. Constant growth and profitability are not a given. There will come a time when companies face the difficult decision of letting workers go. Yet even in such a challenging moment for a company, there are ways to make a difficult situation more palatable.

Consider the example of Cisco Systems. Trying to find a way to let key employees move on without moving away for good, Cisco created an ingenious win-win-win-win opportunity for about eighty of the six thousand employees it laid off in spring of 2001.

In lieu of severance, employees agreed to work for nonprofits and charities while earning just a third of their Cisco salaries but retaining their benefits and stock options. There is no cost to the nonprofits, and the workers get preferential treatment when Cisco starts hiring again.[120] In so doing, Cisco benefits, nonprofits benefit, employees benefit, and the community benefits simultaneously.

TrendSmart **Tips**

- Know your own strengths as well as those of your employees.
- Instill confidence in all employees; make sure they know their abilities are valued.
- Align your employees' skills with the right jobs; make sure they're doing a job they're well suited for.
- Encourage employee training; it's essential to your employees' success within your company as well as to their own future marketability: a true win-win situation!

Chapter 18

Temporary Careers
Where the Career Ladder Has Very Few Rungs

⊕ ⊕ ⊕

"Give me nothing fixed, set, static."
—*D. H. Lawrence*

Helping guide an employee's career presents a never-ending array of challenges for any business leader, especially today. As we have seen, the workforce, like customers, is increasingly fickle, changing jobs and careers with alacrity and regularity. That is the new norm that *TrendSmart* leaders understand well.

Mentoring a younger worker is understandable and in some ways more common. But at senior executive levels, where cost containment and personality issues can be extremely complex, the emerging trend toward temporary careers presents new challenges.

Age Stereotyping

One recent strategy has been the targeting of the salaries and benefits for the youngest and oldest members of the workforce.

For example, the stereotyping of older employees can be found in many nations, especially in the high-tech sectors. A survey of employers found, for example, that only 2 percent would hire an IT applicant with more than ten years of experience; only 13 percent of the respondents aged twenty to thirty would hire anyone over forty; and 47 percent in the survey had never hired anyone over age forty.[121] Other evidence suggests a *decline* in wages associated with prior experience (see chapter 14). Work longer, earn less.

A couple of years ago, the *San Francisco Examiner* described the plight of an American Ph.D. in biophysics, who had been programming computers since the early 1970s. At the time, he had sent out hundreds of résumés and attended dozens of job fairs. He even lowered his salary sights from $50,000 to $40,000—then to the mid-$30,000 range.[122]

There are hundreds of thousands of unfilled software-engineering and computer-programming jobs in the United States. There's no shortage of high-tech workers; there's only a shortage of high-tech workers under the age of thirty-five.

TrendSmart Tip: Age advantages and age discrimination are taking new forms.

Such age discrimination is not unique—quite the contrary. For example, the Institute of Electrical and Electronics Engineers, a Washington-based group with 330,000 members, has found that for every year of age, it takes an unemployed engineer an average of two weeks longer to find a job. In other words, a forty-five-year-old is likely to stay unemployed forty weeks longer than a job seeker who is twenty-five.

Paul Kostek, president of the Institute, says the industry's push for more foreign workers is simply a way to ensure a constant supply of young, cheap labor and to avoid retraining older workers. Basically, foreigners working in America on work visas are "indentured servants, who serve out six-year terms," Kostek says.

The flip side of age discrimination can also be seen with the workloads of the youngest employees in large, powerful companies. Here, the "trial by fire" attitude prevails among employers. The "use them up" model—high-pressure, high-opportunity, high-effort, low per-hour paycheck jobs—is designed for entry-level workers, virtually all of whom are young.

A group of M.B.A. students surveyed, mainly in consulting firms and investment banks, said they had challenging jobs that stretched them. They also reported long hours and high stress.[123] Firms typically took an ambitious employee, added a social environment that created lots of accountability and pressure to perform, and turned them loose…all for entry-level pay—a sure recipe for early burnout.

Twenty-First Century Guilds

Such treatment of old and young workers is not new. Go back to medieval times—to the twelfth and thirteenth centuries—the Middle Ages, before Europe knew of a New World, never mind a "new economy;" back before there were companies, before there were venture capitalists and entrepreneurs. Go back to a time when there were guilds: merchant guilds, which sought to organize and control how business would be done within a given geographic territory, and craft guilds, which formed to establish work standards to protect the interests of the workers. In the medieval world, guilds played a crucial role in organizing commerce, looking after younger and older workers, and in structuring how work got done.

Now, says Thomas Malone, a professor at MIT's Sloan School of Management and founder of the Center for Coordination Science, take a look at the future of commerce and at the structure of how work will get done. Look particularly at the choices that are available to free agents and talented workers, and what you'll discover is the reemergence of guilds, twenty-first-century style.

The rise of guilds is a response to the increasing prevalence of career-hopping, wherein being in a guild offers the individual a sense of community amid change. For a modern example, Malone cites the Screen Actors Guild (SAG). "Guilds are organizations that provide a wide range of services for mobile workers, the kinds of services that employers have traditionally provided. For example, SAG contracts stipulate that producers pay a surcharge into the guild's benefits fund—an amount that can be as much as 30 percent of an actor's base pay. SAG members need to earn only $6,000 in a calendar year to qualify for full health benefits for the entire subsequent year. SAG offers educational and professional development seminars to its members, and, because many actors have relatively short careers, SAG also provides very generous pension benefits."[124]

TrendSmart Tip: Understand the importance of guilds and work-related communities in creatively harnessing the resources of the new workforce of free agents.

Permanent Temps

Though guilds provide a variety of services to their individual members, a growing segment of the workforce still prefers to work as temporary employees. "Permanent temps" are now very common, and they exist as sole proprietorships without the benefit of guild-level support and services. In spite of this, temps often identify a number of factors that make them want to remain free agents:

- More flexibility in work choices
- Exposure to a variety of jobs, managers, and companies
- Constant upgrading and learning of skills
- The ability to balance work, family, and outside interests

Rent-a-Boss

Most people associate "temps" with entry-level or clerical jobs. However, a new industry of "interim workers" has emerged in the past two decades. The practice of employing interim executives—the "rent-a-chief" approach—has grown dramatically and ranks as a multibillion-dollar-a-year industry worldwide.

As we discussed, Marion McGovern has created a thriving San Francisco–based company named M^2, which matches up high-level independent consultants with companies seeking temporary high-level expertise. Her success is made possible by the accelerated specialization of the economy and the desire for workforce flexibility.[125]

At Newgistics, an Austin, Texas, company, the use of interim workers has been taken to new levels. The reverse logistics company deliberately enlisted many senior level, interim executives to be here today, gone tomorrow. No muss, no fuss, and no golden parachutes. Its strategy for profitability, as well as its business plan, was in part built on the premise that permanent interim workers, at all levels of the company, would give them a competitive advantage.[126]

TrendSmart Tip: Use temporary or interim personnel, at all levels of skill and expertise. It is a viable win-win for free agents *and* employers.

Suggestions Anyone?

To any prospective employer, there are many subtle advantages of hiring interim personnel. For example, one such value-add contributed by free agents is their ability to see old things in new ways. With fresh eyes, they are often able to streamline procedures, spot "sacred cows," and suggest cost-saving shortcuts. For this reason, smart companies have created sophisticated channels for gathering and tracking suggestions from employees, new and old.

But we live in an imperfect world, and consequently it is common for many suggestions to be "firehosed" or dismissed prematurely. According to Mark McCormack, founder and CEO of International Management Group, several factors affect the quality and quantity of suggestions, as revealed in an interview by Dave Murphy.

Why are ideas rejected? "Certainly, there are good reasons for turning someone down," says McCormack, "but often a manager's inertia is to blame. Implementing change means more work for managers. If you have a set of overwhelmed or underenergetic managers, fresh ideas will wither away."[127]

People leave their jobs for a variety of reasons, and there can be both a push and a pull. When suggestions are left unacknowledged or are not encouraged for long periods of time, worker loyalty and productivity is undermined. Morale drops, and the circulation of résumés increases.

A disillusioned worker is a prime candidate for a change of jobs. Globally, what we are seeing is a diminishing loyalty, commitment, and longevity of the workforce. The emerging trend, which has migrated from the United States and Europe, is not simply a succession of short-term, high-intensity jobs, but the shifting from one industry and/or career to another.

Career-Hopping

In today's globalized marketplace, the shift is from viewing "job-hopping" as acceptable to viewing "career-hopping" as acceptable as well. A waitress becomes a schoolteacher. A schoolteacher heads up a nonprofit. The nonprofit executive director becomes vice president of human resources at a large private corporation. The human-resources vice president becomes a consultant to the aerospace industry. The consultant writes a book or two. And all of this can happen in the condensed span of two decades.

People have changed jobs about every four years for the past two or three decades, and for many reasons: life choices, family, health, new opportunities, etc. They change careers, too, for similar reasons, and for one additional reason: there is no longer any reason *not* to consider changing careers. In fact, there are many incentives now *to* change careers.

TrendSmart Tip: Take career-hopping as a given.

Career-hopping applies transferable skills in new settings. Career moves take courage and vision, and some high self-esteem, too. Consequently, the prevalence of job and career changes is no longer the warning signal it once was to a hiring manager. In fact, I often hear the reverse: hiring managers wonder what is amiss if an applicant has been at one job for more than four or five years. Nothing is necessarily wrong with applicants who have worked at many companies. Certainly some people "cannot hold a job," but I am not talking about that. I am talking about bright people, people with a sense that the future is theirs to invent.

Of course, when reviewing one hundred or one thousand applicants, you need to look with logic and intuition for something that singles someone out. And you still have to do the due diligence and check references. But you should not reject an applicant solely because of job or career movement. Furthermore, a *TrendSmart* manager sometimes may "push" an employee by saying, "This person should change jobs, and I have just the opening in mind." This is why the role of the human-resources manager today is increasingly part scientist, part artist, and part matchmaker.

TrendSmart Tips

- Age advantages and age discrimination are taking new forms.
- Understand the importance of guilds and work-related communities in creatively harnessing the resources of the new workforce of free agents.
- Use temporary or interim personnel, at all levels of skill and expertise. It is a viable win-win for free agents *and* employers.
- Take career-hopping as a given.

Chapter 19

Complementary Competence

Where Opposite Competencies Attract

⊕ ⊕ ⊕

"Always waiting untold in the souls
of armies of the common people,
is stuff better than anything that can possibly
appear in the leadership of the same."
—*Walt Whitman*

The Peter Principle is alive and kicking, nearly forty years after the creation of the term. Based on a bestselling book of the same name, the Peter Principle says that in many industries and organizations, people initially are promoted and climb the career ladder on the basis of their competencies. Then they are promoted once more—but this time to a position for which they are incompetent. Compounding matters, once the person is moved into a position for which they are incompetent, there they stay—protected and supported by legal and/or organizational policies.

Knowing what you are good at is useful information, but better still, knowing what you are *not* good at—where you are in fact incompetent—is priceless. Unlike many managers who insist upon bolstering and improving weaknesses, *TrendSmart* leaders know that the appropriate ironic strategy today is to surround yourself with others whose strengths complement your weaknesses. Like the children's nursery rhyme—"Jack Sprat could eat no fat, his wife could eat no lean"—*TrendSmart* leaders these days know the fat from the lean, and unabashedly use both.

TrendSmart Tip: Know not only what you're good at but also what you *aren't* good at—and then surround yourself with others whose strengths complement your weaknesses.

These leaders strike a balance between knowing the competencies and the incompetencies of the work team. They are then in the enviable position of being able to match staff members with others whose strongest and weakest points are known and can be factored into the dynamics of a productive environment. I refer to this emerging trend as "complementary competence."

Some companies go so far as to handpick rising stars with a range of strengths and team them up to leverage strengths and minimize weaknesses via the partnership. Unfortunately, most don't.

The Peter Principle Meets the Patler Principle

I have long been puzzled by the longevity and perseverance of the Peter Principle. Recently, it occurred to me that three other "principles" are found nearly as often in the workplace. Visually, they look like Exhibit 19-1.

Exhibit 19-1. The Patler Principle		
	Low Personal Competence	**High Personal Competence**
Low Organizational Support	I. The Throwaway Principle	II. The Judas Principle
High Organizational Support	III. The Peter Principle	IV. The Patler Principle

Let's look at all four.

I. The Throwaway Principle

This is the most common of the four, and the easiest to recognize. Both employer and employee are aware of the unwritten Covenant of Disposability! Typically, Throwaways are young workers on their first job. They are expected by the employer to be on the job a short time, they get sparse training, and the loyalty of both parties is minimal. Those are the rules of this "game." The fast-food industry is especially susceptible to the use of the Throwaway Principle.

**TrendSmart Tip: Avoid the "Throwaway Principle."
Make sure your company doesn't view its young workers
as disposable; instead, give them the training and
mentoring they need to succeed and get ahead.**

II. The Judas Principle

Of all four principles, this one is the most innocent and elusive. In fact, the Judas Principle is so subtle that it is almost imperceptible. This is a situation where you have talented, competent people who are recognized as such by the employer. The problem is, the employer takes them for granted. The employer assumes it does not need to give the same level of support or budget or staffing to maximize such employees' competencies. Consequently, in many situations where I have spotted the Judas principle in operation, clients are genuinely surprised, nearly apologetic, and certainly more than willing to rectify the situation. Left unchecked, however, "betrayal" is present, hence the allusion to the biblical Judas.

TrendSmart Tip: Avoid the "Judas Principle" of management, where companies betray their best and most competent workers by taking them for granted.

III. The Peter Principle

As I mentioned, with the Peter Principle, you have a situation where employees have been competent in many areas but then are promoted into a position for which they are incompetent, ill equipped, or even inept. But there they remain, for a very long time, typically protected by policies and laws. Companies with human-resources policies based on seniority or tenure systems are especially prone to the Peter Principle. Adding insult to injury, it is probably the most damaging to organizations that wish to be quick, agile, and flexible, because they have the wrong people doing the wrong jobs in inept ways for a very long time!

TrendSmart Tip: Beware of the Peter Principle. Make sure you don't overpromote your employees to a level of work they can't handle.

IV. The Patler Principle

The optimal situation is one wherein the organization: identifies employees' competencies and places them in positions where those competencies will flourish; gives them appropriate support; and celebrates their accomplishments. For example, the hospitality industry often follows the Patler Principle when it spots an employee who has tremendous people skills and places that person in face-to-face assignments with guests. As one never to turn down a chance to be involved with a win-win situation, I take the liberty of naming this principle after myself. Vanity has its moments!

TrendSmart Tip: Strive for the "Patler Principle."
Identify your employees' best skills and competencies,
and place them in positions where they can flourish.

Twinning Is Winning

To better understand the Patler Principle, it is useful to know both sides of the same coin. On one side, employees and individuals benefit from knowing—and then building upon—their strengths. That is the most common form of the Patler Principle. More subtle, though, is the "complementary competence" angle, where you seek to pair off an employee with another who has skills that complement his or her competencies.

We see complementary competence working at the highest levels. For example, 55 percent of 2000 *Inc 500* CEOs started their companies with at least one cofounder.[128] Share the work; share the wealth. Consider the following:

- Sean and Scott Smith are twins who have been virtually inseparable since they were born fifteen minutes apart from each other. So it's no surprise that the Smith brothers founded Coalition America together. Their height and hair coloring may be nearly identical, but not much else is when it comes to business…and that is a good thing. Their skills dovetail nicely, with Sean acting as the corporate visionary while Scott oversees the daily operations. Sean claims his CEO status has nothing to do with birth order. "But I am always 15 minutes ahead of my brother," he jokes.[129]

- A Marin County, California, nonprofit created a coexecutive director position. In doing so, the board of directors leveraged the respective strengths of two of its most valued employees. The board decided to promote them both simultaneously, one to run the day-to-day program and the other to handle the job of fund-raising.

- College roommates Rob Johnstone and Gerry Frey founded Priority Express Courier. Johnstone headed up sales while Frey managed the operations. In their case, however, they had multiple competencies and took turns concerning who did what competent work, when. Four years after founding the company, both men were feeling burned out, so they decided to switch roles, figuring it might reinvigorate them and, consequently, the company. The switch must have worked out quite well, as "the two friends have no plans to trade places again."[130]

Balancing Acts

Gustave Flaubert once observed that "Nothing is more humiliating than to see idiots succeed in enterprises we have failed in."[131] Today though, there is an addendum, and sweet revenge, to Flaubert's observation: idiots burn out. In addition to collaborating in the workplace, we all benefit, as well, from finding a corresponding match in our personal lives.

If we only know how to work but take no respite and refreshment from time spent *off* work, our productivity decreases over time. Personal balance—having family, friends, or community who can benefit from our talents and who will pick up in those areas where we don't excel—is the *individual* equivalent of the Patler Principle.

Some companies encourage personal balance. "I had not seen too many people be able to do this thing called balance," explains Herman Miller president and CEO Michael Volkema. "I think society has told us that we have to compartmentalize ourselves, so when we show up for work, you're supposed to leave fatherhood behind, leave motherhood behind; you're supposed to leave your ethnicity and worldviews behind. But several years ago, I concluded that I had to take a different approach. I said, 'Never again will I separate who I am from what I do, and never will I let what I do become who I am.' That's a journey, and I fail from time to time, but it's my mantra."[132]

I have more than once heard CEOs on an acquisition path say, "The only reason to buy another company is for its people."[133] If you do it carefully, you can acquire an entire corporate culture that largely complements your own company culture, creating the *interorganizational* equivalent of the Patler Principle.

TrendSmart Tip: Understand that competent people are the most important element of business success.

A Conversation: The Dichotomies of Leadership

TrendSmart leaders seek out the best practices in any industry and identify the ways in which best practices in one industry can migrate to another. I am, therefore, always on the lookout for leaders and top executives who can provide useful models of the skills needed to meet business challenges. We live in a world of dichotomies, where the ability to address the seemingly contradictory demands placed on leaders becomes a true business asset. So it is appropriate now to turn to a closer examination of some leadership practices that address the emerging trend of complementary competence.

Throughout this book, we have touched upon dozens of companies and more than one hundred individuals to illustrate a wide array of actions taken in the face of emerging trends. In the balance of this chapter, the tables are turned, and we look in some detail at one individual in one company, who faces an array of emerging trends—head on.

Linda Hudson, president of General Dynamics ATP (GDATP), and one of the highest-ranking female executives in the defense industry, is one such example. GDATP, based in Charlotte, North Carolina, is part of the nearly $12 billion parent company, General Dynamics.

I have worked with Linda and her team on several projects and have been impressed by what they have accomplished in a fairly short amount of time. They took a traditional manufacturing company and culture and outsourced manufacturing, reduced employment by 30 percent, acquired a new company, grew sales by 40 percent, and consolidated facilities, all in less than three years. Since GDATP does a number of things very well—and a few things that still need improvement—I will share a recent conversation she and I had in order to highlight a spectrum of ideas and initiatives that I believe are of wide-ranging, interindustry utility to any *TrendSmart* leader.

LP: *Tell me a little about your management approach.*

LH: In order for a leader to talk about a management approach, it is important to understand the environment of the company and the initial problems faced. I believe effective management tools and techniques are very situational, and the successful leader knows when and where to do things differently.

LP: *How were you received upon arrival?*

LH: My selection as president was not without controversy—I was a woman in a traditionally male field. But I believe I was selected because of my proven track record, my ability to understand the performance problems, and my willingness to take action and redefine the future direction of the company. Still, I arrived to face a fearful, skeptical, and demoralized workforce.

LP: *So what did you do right off the bat?*

LH: I did not get rid of the two competitors for my job; they were exceptional individuals, and I gave them the two most senior positions in the company. I then laid out the ground rules for my senior staff at our first staff meeting. I started by talking about "My Style." I told them that I was a traditional manager and decision-maker. I would seek input from them but not consensus. I like to delegate responsibility and authority, and I expect full accountability as a result. I told them I'd also expect and reward superior performance but had no tolerance for insubordination or failure to execute direction. Of course, I reminded them that I was very focused on customers and new business, and therefore my top priorities were the future and strategic thrusts.

LP: *That's a pretty clear and honest set of "tough love" expectations. It must also have signaled to them that change was coming and there was a lot of work to be done, and done in new ways.*

LH: True, and I also told them that I would never ask them to do more or work harder than I was willing to work myself.

LP: *And the savvy ones saw the handwriting on the wall?*

LH: It took a while for everyone to catch on to the new approach. I acted quickly to make senior-management changes at my staff level, but I had even more concerns about the existing leadership at the midmanagement level, primarily because their strengths had not been maximized. I knew the success or failure of the company would depend upon improving the self-esteem and skills of this middle-management group.

LP: *Knowing you, this must have been interesting...how did you do this?*

LH: I chose two primary and very different tacks. First, immediate high-profile job eliminations and demotions (which I now affectionately call "public examples") to establish my authority and to make sure everyone understood that there would be change, accountability, and associated consequences for poor performance and failure to support my initiatives and business objectives.

LP: *OK, that's the bad cop. Tell me about what the good cop did.*

LH: Well, in addition, I placed a highly visible emphasis on leadership development to strengthen the hard and soft skills of management and supervision at all levels throughout the company and, more important, to instill pride in being a key player in the future of the company.

LP: *So, tell me a bit more about the other initiatives you launched. I know you have a group of twelve identified future leaders that you work with for a year at a time, the President's Leadership Development Group.*

LH: This is the most unusual initiative we've undertaken. I wanted to work with a few people to give them the broad exposure and expertise required to be a corporate leader. As I began to plan the program for the group, I tried to define the attributes of the business leaders I most admire. And I usually ended up with the summary that these individuals are interesting and involved people. Yet only once in my career did anyone provide me with an opportunity to develop these attributes for my own professional growth. I have come to believe that the development of social and personal skills is every bit as important in career development as the classic job-specific and management skills, so we developed a program that dealt with all of these aspects.

LP: *So you had an intuitive "profile" of the positive attributes of a future corporate leader…which sounds like the Patler Principle to me.*

LH: In selecting the individuals for this program, I looked for people who had demonstrated exceptional performance. I looked for people with eagerness and a passion to do new things. I looked for individuals that had indicated to me, or to their management, that they wanted a broader role in the company. I selected them from varied organizations, varied backgrounds, different ages, and different types of skill sets because I wanted the group to benefit from their experiences with one another.

The program is a mix of classroom training (approximately 240 hours), specialized job assignments, mentoring, social events, etiquette training, community service, and significant time spent with me and my senior staff. The classroom training includes traditional classes like negotiation skills and professional writing but also addresses less traditional topics like becoming your boss's best friend and how to influence others. Each person has a mentor on my staff, and they selectively participate in my staff meetings and senior-staff off-site meetings. Each individual is required to get involved in a community-service project that interests them.

LP: *That is quite an assortment of things to put on their plate. Was there anything totally unique, in your own mind, about this program?*

LH: A new twist that I haven't ever seen done before in a leadership program is that all of the participants report directly to me during the course of the program—for the whole year. I feel that it is important to structurally remove these individuals from their functional organizations. I want the latitude to put the participants in special assignments when the business needs arise, and becoming their manager requires me to interface more frequently with the participant, which is one of my objectives. Twice a year I have in-depth performance and career discussions with each one of the participants.

LP: *So on a regular basis you are also able to tap into their evolving competencies.*

LH: This program is different from everything else we've done, because it's my personal commitment to make an impact on our future leadership and it is a tailored program intended to grow the skills of an individual. It is also intended to be a public display of talent and an indication of the valued skills and behaviors within the company.

LP: *You know I am fond of asking you what are the "les-*

sons learned" from the things we have worked on together. So tell me, what are the lessons learned from these first three years that might benefit other leaders?

LH: I've learned that it is truly all about people—strong leadership, clear goals, accountability, and rewards. The only absolutes I've discovered are that the pace of change only increases, and that people are the most important element of success.

TrendSmart **Tips**

- Know not only what you're good at but also what you *aren't* good at—and then surround yourself with others whose strengths complement your weaknesses.
- Avoid the "Throwaway Principle." Make sure your company doesn't view its young workers as disposable; instead, give them the training and mentoring they need to succeed and get ahead.
- Avoid the "Judas Principle" of management, where companies betray their best and most competent workers by taking them for granted.
- Beware of the Peter Principle. Make sure you don't overpromote your employees to a level of work they can't handle.
- Strive for the "Patler Principle." Identify your employees' best skills and competencies, and place them in positions where they can flourish.
- Understand that competent people are the most important element of business success.

Chapter 20

Business Casual
Where the Conventional and the Unconventional Meet

⊕ ⊕ ⊕

"Perfect friendship is the friendship of (those)
who are good and alike in excellence."
—*Aristotle*

L est there be any confusion, please take note of the word order of this chapter title. The emerging trend is not "casual business" but rather "business casual." Business today is casual in that it is more flexible, more at ease with change, and more dynamic. In that sense it is more "casual" than formal. A tremendous amount of solid work gets done, and wealth generated, by men wearing polo shirts and women in comfortable slacks. What they all share, as Aristotle observed, is that they are "alike in excellence."

We have moved from organizations built on "tiers and ties"—

stratified, vertical, organizational fortresses run like an "old boys' club" with a rigid dress code to boot—to those that succeed today based more on "deliverables and Dockers." Organizations are flattening and broadening in structure, and the shift in clothing to "business casual" is therefore best understood as the visual convergence of wardrobe and mind-set. Don't be fooled; there is nothing casual about doing business in new ways. Even as ties and suits creep in and out of fashion, the mixture of results-orientation and flexibility of work styles is here to stay.

> **TrendSmart Tip: Business casual is an evolving way of doing business today.**

The Lines Have Blurred

The modern company has, quite literally, a different "look." It is less top-heavy, more flexible, increasingly affected by women, and has a spirit of the classic entrepreneur. The wide range of "dress codes" company to company is only a metaphor for the greater changes in the world of commerce.

"The days of dressing to impress your...clients are over," says a spokesperson for Goldman Sachs. But, he adds, when appropriate, "We do have our bankers keep suits here for meetings."[134]

"Many of our customers represent the heads of the firms," adds Clifford Grodd, president of Paul Stuart. "I've watched their thinking metamorphose. Now they recognize that what the young guys wanted was a palace coup. They recognize that the lines of authority have blurred, that the work effort has slackened. There's no doubt in my mind that the dress code will come back."

Consider the impact of something as basic as dress codes and how they shift and change with the times. They are one window into a changing business world.

Incrementally Challenged

Let's look at some more subtle examples of the nuances of business casual. In examining the dot-com environment, dollarDEX discovered that most prospective employees were looking to cash in on stock options quickly, not to help build a successful organization incrementally. For that reason, founder Richard Lai and his senior managers targeted "old economy" workers who were interested in tasting a bit of the "new economy." To do this, they negotiated with a traditional consulting firm that was losing the battle of departing employees. "Out-ternships" were offered to the consulting firm's staff so that employees could work at dollarDEX for a year, without stock options, and experience the exhilaration of the new economy with no reduction in their consulting-firm salaries.

Poise under fire and staying "cool" became important factors, almost in spite of themselves. "Actually, staying cool is not conventional wisdom," says Lai. "How many times have we heard someone say that in the new economy it's more important to shoot first and then aim? Our strategy is to get above the noise and acquire customers despite massive advertising by our competitors."[135]

Sustainable results are the name of the new game. As every dot-com-turned-*not*-com attests, *repeatable* success is hard to come by, and when examined up close, is always the by-product of refreshed, energized, bright people doing engaging work as part of interesting and balanced lives. To *TrendSmart* leaders then, business "casual" is serious business.

Baseball Caps and Capital

In the business-casual arena, ingenuity is at a premium. For example, the Chicago area, feeling very much outmaneuvered by Silicon Valley on the west coast and Silicon Alley on the east, started its "Silicon

Prairie" initiative. The state sponsored a three-day retreat of the city's venture-capital investors and angels. "The first day of the conference was all old guys standing around in dark suits, trying to sound like they 'got' the Internet," recalls FreeWheelz board member Skip Lehman.

Asked to address one breakout session of bankers and real-estate investors, Lehman came in a rumpled white shirt, jeans, and a baseball cap with a hole for his ponytail. He clapped everyone to attention and said, "I'm told that in the new economy, if you don't have an idea, you should wear a suit. At least you look smart. Well, I don't have a good suit, but I've got a hell of an idea." Then he whipped off the baseball cap, to which his ponytail was sewn. "Now that I've got your attention," he continued, "let me tell you how you can all get rich and possibly get a free car to boot." By the end of the conference, Lehman had $15 million to start his business.

The story does not end there. Two days after the conference, Felix Atchison called Skip Lehman with an offer he couldn't refuse. "I basically told him I wanted to be president of his company and that he'd be an asshole not to take me."[136] There are times when the total absence of subtlety has its intrinsic value.

Adults Wanted, Experience Preferred

"Look at Internet companies that have had success over the past several years, like Yahoo! or AOL," says Priceline.com founder and vice chairman Jay Walker. "These companies are run by adults who take a long-term view of building substantial, profitable franchises. The market isn't saying anything different from what it was saying two years ago. It's still looking for models that are sustainable. The business press talks to itself and amplifies the self-reinforcing effect of the fashion du jour, but most investors, as opposed to traders, are still investing in companies for the long term."[137]

**TrendSmart Tip: Increasingly, the mix of
fresh energy and seasoned experience are viable
components of any lasting endeavor.**

You Are What (and Whom) You Value

As we have seen, a company's core values are often essential to its success. Charles O'Reilly and Jeffrey Pfeffer, authors of *Hidden Value*, point out that "no one can be very motivated if they genuinely believe that what they are doing is worthless." While they readily admit that "the notion of corporate values seems like just another management fad," they also point out that a company has values whether it frames them and hangs them on the wall or not. "The only question is how explicit they are about them," they say. "Too often, these implicit values take the form of 'follow orders,' 'please your boss,' 'don't take risks,' 'don't fail,' and 'act in your own best interest, because the organization won't.'"[138]

"Companies that value their employees as people," comments Suzannah Clark, "not simply as economic agents, respect their employees for who they are instead of just what they do, and they build a community of people who share similar beliefs and unleash the potential of every person in their workforce."

"The reason the kind of success won by these companies is so hard to reproduce in other companies," say O'Reilly and Pfeffer, "is that heads of companies have a difficult time trusting and believing in their employees....The only way a competitor could replicate these [values] would be to truly believe in them and to consistently behave in accordance with them."

My firm belief is that it's not how many ideas come out of one's mind, but how many dollars come out of the ideas. That is one difference between creativity (generating ideas) and innovation (making them implementable and profitable). Ideas are a dime a dozen, but the million-dollar idea comes from solid trend information and good, old-fashioned thinking put to practical use.

These days, thinking needs to be three-dimensional as well as practical. As Julie Bick asks in *All I Really Need to Know in Business I Learned at Microsoft,* "Can you learn to think three moves ahead? Don't just focus on what you'll do to set your business apart, but think about how your competitor will counter your move. Then develop a contingency plan to deal with whatever they'll throw back at you."[139] Microsoft, for all its critics, has certainly been quite adept at this kind of preemptive thinking.

Good thinking is hard work. Since this book is filled with hundreds of ideas and trends and best practices, the reader is reminded that the real challenge is to remain focused and yet find balance in your life. It can be as simple as changing your job title to one that motivates you to action. And what's in a name? Part of the business-casual style is pushing the boundaries of the conventional decorum for job titles within the context of a company's culture. Consider these three out-of-the-box examples:

- **Title: Reality Facilitator**
  Who: Jan Darwin
  Company: Lexica Holdings LLC
  Previous title: Administrative assistant at Charles Schwab[140]
- **Title: Raging Inexorable Thunder-Lizard Evangelist for Change**
  Who: Brian Yeoman
  Company: Health Science Center, University of Texas, Houston[141]
  Previous title: Assistant vice president for support services

- **Title: Web Archaeologist**
  Who: Michelle Friedman
  Company: Organic Online, Inc.
  Previous title: Web developer, MicroWarehouse[142]

The Tortoise Wins

In the private business sector, conventional wisdom holds that the ultimate goal is profitability. Then came the great dot-com era, where profitability took a backseat so long as venture capital was thrown at a company or shareholders had confidence in its stock valuation. But after a few years, shareholders and investors lost confidence in those who lost money hand over fist.

In the aftermath of the dot-com bomb, Internet-based firms that actually make money are crowing—even if profits are slender. The absurdity of the situation was revealed in a press release from Seattle's Wildpartygames.com, which recently trumpeted its quarterly results: sales of $2,620; net profit of $335.[143] Well, at least it's a start—and via some clever guerrilla marketing, they got their Net address in a newspaper column (and this book), which is probably what they wanted to do anyway. The fact that newspapers nationwide in the United States ran the story is itself an indication of what the public understanding of dot-coms has come to. "We are not expecting to get rich quick," Chief Executive Officer Brian Pellham said. "Doesn't the tortoise win the race anyway?"

From Start to Finnish

Things change. But even when things change, there are some constants. Good thinking, good strategy, good information remain at a premium. Today, the scale of change can be staggering, wherein some *corporations* change more quickly than their host *nations*. In the last couple of years, for example, Finnish teenagers have quit referring to mobile phones as *jupinalle*—"yuppie teddy bears"—and started calling them *kännykkä* or *känny,* a Nokia trademark that passed into generic parlance and means "an extension of the hand."[144] The shift in name reflects a deeper shift, from seeing a new technology as a toy to seeing it as a necessity, even as an extension of the body.

The role—even the necessity—of some technologies is worth tracking and analyzing. Comparisons and telling facts are valuable mechanisms for gaining insights. Recently, for example, more mobile phones were sold worldwide than automobiles and personal computers combined. Nokia alone employs many more engineers than all of Finland.

Technology is neutral. It can foster and lead change or be a mere tool. For example, analog cellular was the *first* wave, and digital networks the *second.* The *third* generation of data and voice communications—the convergence of mobile phones and the Internet, high-speed wireless data access, intelligent networks, and pervasive computing—will shape how we work, shop, pay bills, flirt, keep appointments, conduct wars, keep up with our children, and write poetry in the next century

Casual work styles do not mean you are not working. A friend of principal research fellow for the Helsinki Telephone Corporation Risto Linturi tells how she once called him to talk business when he was walking his dog. Curious, she asked if he was working. "Of course I'm working," he replied. "I'm *thinking.*"

Forces at Work

The ability to forecast and foresee the immediate and emerging future is part demographics, part dreams. As someone who has spent more than twenty years in the world of trend analysis, I know that you win some and you lose some in terms of the accuracy of your trend forecasts. Because of inherent contradictions, predictions have an odd and short half-life, even when made by astute observers such as Kevin Kelly. In 1999, he said, "It may be that *at this particular moment* in our history, the convergence of a demographic peak, a new global marketplace, vast technological opportunities, and financial revolution will unleash two uninterrupted decades of growth."[145] Within days of his writing this, the dot-com slide was in full tilt, and within two years the world was fully engulfed in the impact of an economic slowdown.

Yet we must not throw the proverbial baby out with the bath water, for writers like Kelly often have wonderful insights and structures of the mind, even though some of their conclusions do not play out. Let me summarize Kelly's observation that the economy reflects four forces at once.

Demographic Peak

The largest, best-educated, most prosperous generation that has ever lived is entering its peak years of productivity, earning, and spending. This is true for the United States, but also for much of the rest of the developed world. This boom of producers and consumers creates a huge market for products, a huge force of creativity, a huge pile of money, and a huge demand for investments.

Technology Rush

The largest deployment of novel products and services, labor-saving machines, and life-changing techniques is now under way. In addition, Kelly says, we'll begin to harvest the productivity gains of technology deployed in the past two decades. But most important, new technology is creating entirely new territories of economic development (the Internet and kin) that will be profitably settled in the next decade.

Financial Revolution

Money itself is undergoing a revolution. The velocity of money—how often it changes hands—continues to increase, he says. Middle-class values continue to spread around the world, while financial inventions continue to proliferate. "Innovations such as mutual funds, rapid IPOs, microloans, twenty-four-hour markets, hedge funds, smart-cards, reverse auctions, and mass online trading," says Kelly, "liberate the flow of capital and spur intense economic growth. And the transformation of money and markets has only just begun."

Global Openness

The spread of democracy, open markets, freedom of speech, and consumer choice around the globe accelerate economic growth. Global openness not only enlarges the potential market for any invention to five billion customers, argues Kelly, it also creates intense competition among governments to construct environments hospitable to progress. Prosperity can no longer be segregated to one part of the globe, and when prosperity does break out, it is amplified quickly by ever-spreading freedoms. Startling statistics support such observations. Today, eight million Americans are millionaires. Ultra-prosperity should push the number of millionaires living next door to about sixteen million in another decade, and about thirty million by 2020. In twenty years, there could be one company for every three Americans, and the emerging trend of business casual will drive this change.

The End of Economic Adolescence

Of course, success is not an entitlement program, and it will not come easily. Even with a changing dress code, it is still necessary to roll up one's sleeves and *work*. *TrendSmart* leaders know that the "rosy" and the "blurry" must both be understood and strategically accounted for. Astute observers, like Daniel Pink, look soberly at the present in light of recent history and paint a less optimistic picture. Three developments, he argues, have "catapulted talented individuals to the center of the story…and will keep them there in the coming chapters."[146]

First, economic adolescence is over. The Organization Man of the 1950s and 1960s worked in an economic climate warmed by the sun of corporate paternalism. Giant companies such as AT&T ("Ma Bell"), Kodak ("The Great Yellow Father"), and Metropolitan Life ("Mother Met") promised to take care of their workers. But in the late 1980s and early 1990s, when globalization and technology squeezed those companies, "they booted out their employees like wayward teenagers."

Curiously, dot-com companies revived the family metaphor— only this time Mother and Father were like the cool parents down the block, "the ones you always wished were yours," says Pink. Plus, good and not-so-old MomAndDad.com gave the kids a huge allowance. They let them have a dog. They turned the office into a rumpus room. And when times toughened? They booted out the kids. The lesson: this economy is rated strictly for adults.

Second, workers now own the means of production. In the industrial economy, the tools necessary to create wealth were too expensive for one person to purchase, too cumbersome for one person to operate, and too large for one person to house. Until the 1980s, for example, a sophisticated computer might require a large air-conditioned room for optimal performance. Not anymore. Today, the tools necessary to create wealth—for example, the laptop computer on which I wrote this book—are easy for a lone individual to purchase, operate, and house. So why *would* that lone individual want to share the profits that he or she is creating? The lesson: organizations need individuals more than individuals need organizations.

Third, corporate lifespans are shrinking. Remember a little outfit called Netscape? Netscape was formed in 1994, went public in 1995, and was gone by 1999, subsumed into AOL's operation. This giant of the new economy reached only its fourth birthday. Does this mean that the half-life of companies is falling exponentially? Not really. Perhaps there is a bigger question: was Netscape ever really a company at all, or was it really just an extremely cool project?

Here's what does matter. That short-lived entity put several products on the market, prompted powerful companies (notably Microsoft) to shift strategies, and equipped a few thousand individuals with experience, wealth, and connections that they could bring to their next project. The lesson: people, not companies, are increasingly what is "built to last." Besides, most of us, from Taipei to Toronto to Tokyo to Topeka, will outlast any organization for which we work. Ironic, but true.

The Pendulum Principle

Business casual is now a *way* of working. It is a way of thinking and a way of mixing the conventional with the unconventional. As Susan Greco points out, the so-called "new economy," though the recent object of ridicule and disdain by many, has offered some strategic lessons and pointed out some significant myths of the "old" economic order.[147]

TrendSmart Tip: There are lessons to be learned, pro and con, from the meteoric dot-com era.

Myth #1: "Grow Fast or Die Hard"

A proliferation of hype has led to new imperatives for survival: grow as fast as possible or perish; raise maximum cash—now; empower your employees to be like entrepreneurs. As poet Gertrude Stein said, "There is no answer. There never was an answer. There never will be an answer. That's the answer."

Office Depot bought into the "grow like crazy" myth, ramping up in 1993 to take on selling to large corporations. "I thought we would be able to leverage Office Depot's buying clout and reputation, and get this commercial business cranked up and rocking," said Mark Begelman, former president of Office Depot. "I thought it would be a challenge that we could quickly overcome. Instead, it gave me a big headache." Speaking of his new startup music-products retail business, today he has a new appreciation for the principle of moderation: "I will be less inclined to acquire and more inclined to build from the bottom up."

Myth #2: "You Must Be Virtual."

Susan Sargent, CEO of Susan Sargent Designs and also the wife of business guru Tom Peters, started a top-notch home-furnishings company in 1996. Desiring to retain the lifestyle of an artist, she set up shop in a barn near her Vermont home and planned to outsource all staff, creating a virtual company united by technology rather than real estate. She began by outsourcing her entire sales operation, linking a distant sales manager and 120 independent reps by phone and email. To her dismay, it was a disaster. "They weren't savvy with laptops," she said, and they never jelled as a group.

The company now has six customer-service people under one roof. Today, her attitude has changed. Virtual companies just don't work, she says: "Not when you're evolving madly every day. I can't see any substitute for having everyone in one place."

Myth #3: "Go Global."

Morningstar, Inc. of Chicago publishes financial information and research. In 1994, they opened an office in London, expecting to emulate companies they had read about that had grown beyond their wildest dreams by taking their formulas for success overseas. "We figured we'd just put an ad in the London paper and start selling," said chairman Joe Mansueto.

The experience was a costly one. After eighteen months of unexpected expenses, regulatory roadblocks, and having to build a new database of mutual fund ratings ("You can't just take mutual-fund ratings to another country and start selling them"), they decided to cut losses and close up shop. The lesson: breaking into foreign markets is a complicated business. There are whole new sets of rules to master. Venturing out once again into foreign markets in 1998, the company sought out local help and found a win-win. "Local partners will put up a lot of capital in exchange for the Morningstar know-how," says Mansueto.

Myth #4: "Capital Is Easy."

In the mid-1990s, Fulcrum Direct, a children's clothing retailer, planned to raise megamillions from the private and public markets. CEO Scott Budoff and his managers became experts at unearthing money from every financing source imaginable, starting with friends and family and moving on to angels, institutional investors, banks, factors, corporations, and strategic partners. The pending IPO was like an insatiable monster, eating an "exorbitant amount of the management team's time and resources."

Then, in 1998, "We were advised the market no longer had any interest in small cap deals at that time," Budoff said. He's taken away several lessons. "There's no such thing as easy capital in any market." Even money from friends and family "is very expensive because of the relationships and the expectations." Another lesson: when you're focused so much on raising capital, he warns, "you're spending a lot of time on something very important to your business but which has nothing to do with your business." Perhaps Budoff learned a lesson my mother always told me: gifts are very expensive!

Myth #5: "Everybody Is an Entrepreneur."

San Francisco strategic Internet consultancy Adjacency planned megagrowth by treating all employees as if they were partners. All were given equity stakes, and the most intimate details of the company were openly revealed to employees. That was the plan, at least. The reality was quite different. "We overestimated our employees' desire to be entrepreneurs, and sometimes we scared them," says CEO Andrew Sather. "They didn't want to hear about the company's close calls with missing payroll," Sather admits. "We've learned to filter some information that employees find disconcerting." They also overestimated their staff's ability to keep secrets. After nearly losing a hot new client because of an employee's loose lips, now they're careful to identify what information is top secret. "We've learned to get a lot more explicit about how information can be used," Sather says.

Myth #6: "Technology Makes Life Easier."

At first, Florida special-effects company Cinnabar skyrocketed to success while relying on technology and cyberspace interactions. Then when business dropped off, CEO Johnathan Katz had an epiphany: "My people had become complacent and too reliant on the conveniences of electronic communication like faxes, email, and telephones." So Katz asked his people to put away their electronic toys and pay personal visits to directors, producers, and art directors at production companies. The orders were clear: "Network. Do lunch. Circulate. Go to shoots." The resultant business upsurge confirmed his hunch.

Myth #7: "You Must Be on the Web in a Big Way."

In 1996, clothing cataloger J. Peterman put his entire catalog online. Customers were underwhelmed, and the effort was a flop. It took so long to download images that "I couldn't even stand it—and it was my own catalog!" says CEO J. Peterman. The lesson he learned was an important one: there is a high price for early adoption—and no penalty for waiting for technology to improve. Besides, the old technologies are still working fine in conjunction with new ones. "I get three hundred to four hundred letters a week," he says. "I get only twenty to thirty emails, and half of those talk about the print catalog," he says.

The Drucker Principle: "Too Good is Not Good"

Peter Drucker, one of my favorite business thinkers, understands intuitively the impact of good information, and has made a career from his cogent, sage observations. "For the first time in human history," he says, "people can expect to outlive the organizations that they work for."[148] The implications of this are profound. As we live longer and work for more years, says Drucker, we risk becoming "too good" at what we do. Work that felt challenging when we were in our thirties may feel dull when we reach our fifties—at which point we have twenty years left in our careers. I call this phenomenon the Drucker Principle.

TrendSmart Tip: Most individuals will now outlive the companies they work for.

An old client of his told him, "I know too much about this industry, and everything I know is about yesterday."

"His knowledge is an obstacle; it no longer applies to today's business world," says Drucker.

So, we can see that business casual is anything but casual. As a blend of old and new practices, it is one of the "working contradictions" of today's business world.

TrendSmart Tip: Sometimes, being "too good" at something is not so good.

TrendSmart **Tips**

- Business casual is an evolving way of doing business today.
- Increasingly, the mix of fresh energy and seasoned experience are viable components of any lasting endeavor.
- There are lessons to be learned, pro and con, from the meteoric dot-com era.
- Most individuals will now outlive the companies they work for.
- Sometimes, being "too good" at something is not so good.

Chapter 21

Working Contradictions

Where Contrarian Trends Join Hands

⊕ ⊕ ⊕

"…to dream takes no effort
to think is easy
to act is more difficult
but for a man to act after he has taken thought, this!
is the most difficult thing of all."

—*Charles Olson, poet*

I have saved the most inclusive trend of all for the final chapter. "Working contradictions" accurately summarizes a lesson learned in my many years of trend analysis and consulting. Metaphorically speaking, most trends slip into the workplace through the back door or a small opening in the window. They do not show up, bigger than life, at the reception desk and announce their arrival. To mix metaphors, they come from somewhere out of left field and plop down at your front door, often before you realize it. And, if they are *real* trends, they hang around for a *long* time.

The L/R Game

On a recent plane flight, I had a fascinating conversation with corporate securities expert Marci Rae Blue. She told me about how curiosity has affected her career in positive ways. "And how did you develop that curiosity?" I asked

"When I was in high school my best girlfriend and I used to get up on Saturdays after an overnight and play 'The L/R Game.' We would pick a number over twenty," she explained, "and take turns picking either an 'L' or an 'R'—left or right. We would then write down the sequence of Ls and Rs, get in her dad's car, and follow that route. We had no idea where we were going to end up, but we did like the energy of heading out for the day not knowing where we were going!"

As a travel strategy, I told her, that works well. But, too often, the L/R Game is how business leaders run their companies. They go left or right with too little information too late. If you are *TrendSmart*, you know the proverbial turns in the road before others do, and though you may not have been down that road before, the arrival is all the sweeter, and more profitable!

By their nature, trends initially are anomalies, exceptions to the rules, contradictions to the tried and true. A trend is a trend in part because it *is* a working contradiction. The irony, of course, is that in the workplace these working contradictions are often the source of innovation, comparative advantage, growth, and progress. They are the fuel for the fires of commerce.

Lessons Learned

TrendSmart leaders use a variety of tools and talents for the benefit of their customers, staff, and shareholders. Yet understanding the power of trends is only a starting point. As leaders, they must constantly be looking for the next "big idea" that will give direction in an uncertain world. "Big ideas," as we have seen, are generated by the emergence *and* convergence of trends. When the idea is clear and focused, it can then be reflected in the brand "road map," and it can deliver on the promise of the brand through quality products and exceptional service.

Trends Mingle

Trends do not exist in a vacuum. They mingle and meander and scoot from place to place and industry to industry. Trends are known because of their impact upon events, markets, and people like you and me. Ultimately, any book about trends is of necessity a book about the behavior, values, and needs of people.

As we have seen, trends also do not exist in isolation. In this book I have offered you a brief glimpse of twenty-one trends, any two or more of which, at any point in time, may occur simultaneously. Mathematically speaking, the number of possible combinations is very high, and the number of business opportunities that accrue from being *TrendSmart* is even higher.

Finally, trends have a *cumulative* impact. They combine in ways that make the combination more than the sum of the parts.

Leaders, Customers, Employees

To describe what trends are and how they come to life, this book looked at the impact of trends on three groups of people: leaders, customers, and employees—the lifeblood of commerce. By becoming *TrendSmart*, companies and individuals understand how trends are likely to affect the business model used, and the scope of opportunity in the future. For example, a trend such as "episodic loyalty" has significance, but when linked with the trends of "mass customization" and "selective service" therein lies the *real* power. By developing *TrendSmart* strategies, companies are able to use customized trend research to extend client loyalty.

I have spotted, mapped, and analyzed trends for more than twenty years. To me, knowing and understanding trends is not an abstraction. It has put food on the table, helped client companies grow, and driven innovation and leadership practices that work in charted and uncharted waters alike. For me to make *you* more *TrendSmart, I* must be *TrendSmart* too. The *TrendSmart* quest is, in a word, incessant.

Trends Linked to Strategy, Strategy to Sustainable Success

From beginning to end, I have proposed that trends not put to use in the marketplace are little more than mental exercises. When trend analysis is linked to strategy formation, and strategy formation is tied to new products or services, the leveraging of trend information becomes a solid basis of a competitive advantage. The *TrendSmart* leader, therefore, is one who is consistently in the right place at the right time, and this by design is not accidental.

This is not easy to do, but the many companies and individuals noted in these pages give you, I trust, a starting point in the real world. The good news is that a real trend is a lasting trend, and the return on investment is very high. *TrendSmart* business, marketing, human resources, and sales strategies, like an art treasure, accrue value with age.

In the vocabulary of this book, an emerging trend is a breeding ground for "big ideas." Big ideas, when linked to strategy, new products, and brand road maps have discernable impact upon the bottom line. And a trend that is spotted early on and built into strategy and put into action by *TrendSmart* leaders is a sure route to sustainable success.

The future is, to the *TrendSmart* leader, much like a good friend. There for you when needed most. An incessant ally. A source of strength and continuity.

In uncertain times, what more can you ask for?

Notes

1   "Tree-Killing Mushroom Is Largest Living Thing Ever Found," *The Garden Island* (August 6, 2000): 6-A.

2   Karen Southwick, "The End of the Fare," *Forbes ASAP* (February 21, 2000): 92.

3   "Entrepreneur Profile," *San Francisco Business Times* Reprint (December 26, 1997–January 1, 1998)

4   Heath Row, "Great Harvest's Recipe for Growth," *Fast Company* (December 1998): 46.

5   Polly La Barre, "What's New, What's Not," *Fast Company* (January 1999): 73–81.

6   Steve Silberman, "Just Say Nokia," *Wired* (September 1999): 140.

7   Scott Kirsner, "The Legend of Bob Metcalfe," *Wired* (November 1998): 185, 232–234.

8   "Laying Down the Laws," *Forbes ASAP* (February 21, 2000): 97–100.

9   Louis Patler, "Switching Strategies," *Business: The Ultimate Resource* (New York: Perseus Books Group, 2002).

10 Suzy Wetlaufer, "The Business Case against Revolution," *Harvard Business Review* (February 2001): 113–119.

11 "*Inc.* 500—The List: The 2000 Ranking of the Fastest-Growing Private Companies in America," *Inc. 500* (October 2000): 134.

12 Ibid., 142.

13 Bill Breen, "Full House," *Fast Company* (January 2001): 118–130.

14 Tamar Asedo Sherman, "Nap for Success," *USA Weekend* (June 9–11, 2000): 11.

15 Ron Lieber, "Lessons from America's New Entrepreneurs," *USA Weekend* (August 21–23): 4–5.

16 Daniel H. Pink, "Who Has the Next Big Idea?" *Fast Company* (September 2001): 108–116.

17 Lori Stacy, "Agency for Change," *American Way,* (May 15, 2001): 80–83.

18 *Fast Company* (December 1998): 30.

19 Phillip Britt, "Overcome the Generation Gap," *Business Advisor* (March/April 2000): 4.

20 Louis Patler, *If It Ain't Broke…BREAK IT!* (New York: Warner Books, 1991).

21 David Beardsley, "Don't Have a Cow—Kill One," *Fast Company* (August 1998): 68.

22 Daniel H. Pink, "The Talent Market," *Fast Company* (August 1998): 87–92.

23 Marion McGovern and Dennis Russell, *A New Brand of Expertise* (Woburn, Mass.: Butterworth-Heinemann, 2001).

24 Pat Lencioni, *Five Temptations of a CEO* (San Francisco: Jossey-Bass, 1998).

25 Dave Murphy, "Resisting Temptation," *San Francisco Examiner* (February 28, 1999): J-1–2.

26 Reed Abelson, "Top Exec Shattered the Glass Ceiling at Hewlett-Packard," *San Francisco Examiner* (August 22, 1999): B-1, B-4.

27 Brent Schlender, "The Bill & Warren Show," *Fortune* (July 20, 1998): 51–64.

28 Nigel Williamson, "From a Mud House to a Million," *High Life* (December 1999): 56.

29 "*Inc.* 500—The List," 145 (see note 11 above).

30 George Gendron, "Revenge of the Old Rules," *Inc.* (February 1999): 9.

31 Jim Chilsen, "Life Sounds Pretty Good for Koss Again," *Marin Independent Journal* (August 24, 1998): C3.

32 Andy Law, *Creative Company* (New York: John Wiley & Sons, 1999), as quoted in Lori Stacy, "Agency for Change," *American Way* (May 15, 2001): 81.

33 Samuel Fromartz, "How to Get Your First Great Idea," *Inc.* (April 1998): 91.

34 Elizabeth Weise, "Xerox Research Center Offers Look into Future," *Marin Independent Journal* (October 11, 1999): C2.

35 Clayton M. Christensen, *The Innovator's Dilemma: When New Technologies Cause Great Firms to Fail* (Cambridge, Mass.: Harvard Business School Press, 1997).

36 Fromartz, "Great Idea," 91 (see note 33 above).

37 Bill Robinson, "The DollarDEX Difference," *Hemispheres* (July 2001): 28.

38 Anna Muoio, "Sales School," *Fast Company* (November 1998): 114–115.

39 Curtis Sittenfeld, "The Next Big Things?" *Fast Company* (December 1998): 42.

40 Ibid.

41 Salina Khan, "Personal Service Gets New Standard," *USA Today* (November 8, 1999): 12B.

42 Dewitt Jones, *Everyday Creativity* (videocassette) 2000, www.starthrower.com

43 Gina Imperato, "How to Hire the Next Michael Jordan," *Fast Company* (December 1998): 212–219.

44 "*Inc.* 500—The List," 149 (see note 11 above).

45 Beth Kwon, "You Call This Work?" *FSB* (October 2000): 66.

46 Mark Halper, "It's not a job, It's an Adventure," *Fast Company* (January 1999): 54.

47 Julie Greenberg, "Lynn Hill Breaks the Law of Gravity," *Wired* (November 1998): 122.

48 Jane Ciabattari, "All You Have to Do Is Try," *Parade Magazine* (May 27, 2001): 8.

49 Cheryl Dahle, "From Hacker to Mentor," *Fast Company* (November 1998): 80.

50 Charles Platt, "What's the Big Idea?" *Wired* (September 1999): 122–132.

51 "*Inc.* 500—The List," 155 (see note 11 above).

52 Peter Drucker, *Innovation and Entrepreneurship: Practice and Principles* (New York: Harper & Row Publishers, 1985), as quoted in John Case, "The Power of Innovation," *State of Small Business 2001,* (May 15, 2001): 103–104.

53 Silberman, "Just Say Nokia," 144 (see note 6 above).

54 Steve Bjerklie, "Bed Rock," *San Francisco Metropolitan* in MetroActive online (November 1997).

55 David H. Freedman, "Intensive Care," *Inc.* (February 1999): 72–80.

56 Christopher Selland, "The Role of Technology in CRM," *The Journal of Customer Loyalty* Q4 (2000): 11.

57 Anna Muoio, "The Experienced Customer," *Net Company* (Fall 1999): 26.

58 John Cunniff, "Companies Underestimate the Cost of Losing Workers," *San Francisco Chronicle* (May 30, 1999): J-2.

59 Anita Roddick, "Next Stop—the 21st Century," *Fast Company* (September 1999): 115.

60 Silberman, "Just Say Nokia," 144 (see note 6 above).

61 Robert Jones, *The Big Idea* (New York: HarperBusiness/Harper-Collins, 2000), as quoted in "Towards the Big Idea," Brandweek.online (December 4, 2000): This summary is entirely my responsibility.

62 James Collins and Jerry Porras, *Built to Last* (New York: HarperCollins, 1994).

63 Mike Moser, *United We Brand* (Cambridge, Mass.: Harvard Business School Press, 2003).

64 Muoio, "Sales School," 112 (see note 38 above).

65 "Cheat Sheet," *Fast Company* (November 1998).

66 Susan Greco, "The Best Little Grocery Store in America," *Inc.* (June 2001): 54–61.

67 Muoio, "Sales School," 108 (see note 38 above).

68 Adam Bryant, "Why Flying Is Hell," *Newsweek* (April 23, 2001): 34–47.

69 Gilda Gallop-Goodman, "Ms. Fix-It," *American Demographic* (September 2000): 14–18.

70 Muoio, "Sales School," 112 (see note 38 above).

71 "Red Robin Honors Unbridled Acts of Imagination, Caring and Service," Red Robin restaurant publication (2000).

72 Celine Fitzgerald and Edward Hickman, "Mobile Without Moving," *The Journal of Customer Loyalty,* Q4 (2000): 14.

73 Letter to the editor, *Fast Company* (January 1999): 26.

74 Matthew Boyle, "Beware the Killjoy," *Fortune* (July 23, 2001): 265.

75 Christopher Selland, "The Role of Technology in CRM," *The Journal of Customer Loyalty,* Q4 (2000): 10.

76 Bob Tedeschi, "You May Already Be a Winner," *Wired* (September 1999): 161.

77 Constantine von Hoffman, "Look Before You Leap," *The Industry Standard* (March 19, 2001): 102–103.

78 Bill Breen, "Where Are You on the Talent Map?" *Fast Company* (September 2000): 102–108.

79 Dave Murphy, "A New Attitude," *San Francisco Chronicle* (May 30, 1999): J-1–2.

80 Maggie Jackson, "Bold, Brash GenX Forcing Firms to Adapt," *Marin Independent Journal* (February 8, 2001): C2.

81 Ibid.

82 Brent Schlender, "Pixar's Fun House," *Fortune* (July 23, 2001): 266.

83 Jackson, "Bold, Brash," C2 (see note 80 above).

84 Ibid.

85 Breen, "Talent Map," 102–108 (see note 78 above).

86 Imperato, "Michael Jordan," 212–219 (see note 43 above).

87 Cunniff, "Companies Underestimate," J-2 (see note 58 above).

88 von Hoffman, "Look," 102–103 (see note 77 above).

89 Author unknown, "A Full Life," *The Economist* (September 4, 1999): 65–68.

90 David DeCapua, "The Best Things in Life Are Free," *Inc.* (August 1999): 112.

91 Carol Kleiman, "Firms Retool Benefits for Workers without Families," *Marin Independent Journal* (December 27, 1998): E-1.

92 Robert Trigaux, "Titles Are the New New Thing (Just Call Him Big Kahuna)," *San Francisco Chronicle* (December 17, 2000): J2.

93 Charles O'Reilly III and Jeffrey Pfeffer, *Hidden Value* (Boston: Harvard Business School Press, 2000), as quoted in Susannah Clark, "People Power," *Continental,* (January 2001): 91.

94 Ibid.

95 Ibid.

96 Ibid.

97 Ibid.

98 Bob Rosner, "More Than One Minute," *The Costco Connection* (July 2000): 14–16.

99 George Mason University survey, as quoted in James Feldman, *Celebrate Customer Service* (1999): 50.

100 Britt, "Generation Gap," 4 (see note 19 above).

101 R. Brayton Bowen, *Recognizing and Rewarding Employees* (New York: McGraw-Hill, 2000).

102 Dave Murphy, "Sells Like Team Spirit," *San Francisco Chronicle* (April 8, 2001): J1–J2.

103 Matthew Boyle, "Beware the Killjoy," *Fortune* (July 23, 2001): 268.

104 "The Cure for Pep Talk," *Your Company* (July/August 1999): 26.

105 "Positively Quotable," *Selling Power* (May 2001): 22.

106 Bob Rosner, "Creative Management," *The Costco Connection* (December 2000): 24.

107 Gina Imperato, "How to Hire the Next Michael Jordan," *Fast Company* (December 1998): 212–219.

108 Michael McNeal, "Careers—Michael McNeal," *Fast Company* (December 1998): 122–126.

109 Bill Kramer, "Carolyn's Kids," *Pacific Sun* (July 4–10, 2001): 15.

110 David Beardsley, "These Tests Will Give You Fits," *Fast Company* (November 1998): 88–90.

111 "Red Robin" (see note 71 above).

112 Leigh Buchanan, "The Taming of the Crew," *Inc.* (August 1999): 25.

113 Amy Joyce, "It's Not Just About You Anymore," *San Francisco Chronicle* (April 8, 2001): J1–J2.

114 Jerry Useem, "A Manager for all Seasons," *Fortune* (April 30, 2001): 66–72.

115 Jim O'Connell, "Boozer's Return Strengthens Duke," *Press Democrat* (March 22, 2001): C-8.

116 Robinson, "DollarDEX," 26 (see note 37 above).

117 Bob Rosner, "Creative Management," *The Costco Connection* (December 2000): 24.

118 Clark, "People Power," 91 (see note 138 above).

119 Donna Fenn, "Corporate Universities for Small Companies," *Inc.* (February 1999): 95–96.

120 Karen A. Davis, "Cisco Pays Laid-Off Employees to Work at Nonprofits for Year," *Marin Independent Journal* (September 4, 2001): B6.

121 Peter Cappelli, "Organized against Age," *Purple Squirrel* (May 2001): 18.

122 Mark Helm, "The Computer Age," *San Francisco Examiner* (August 22, 1999): B-5, B-7.

123 Cappelli, "Organized," 18 (see note 121 above).

124 Jill Rosenfeld, "Free Agents in the Olde World," *Fast Company* (May 2001): 136–140.

125 Tom Ehrenfeld, "Just Managing: The Ironic Economy," *The Industry Standard* (2000).

126 Gardner Selby, "Executive Temps," *Southwest Airlines Spirit* (February 2001): 30–32.

127 Dave Murphy, "Companies Need to Pay Attention to Those Little Voices Within," *San Francisco Chronicle* (April 8, 2001): J1–J2.

128 "*Inc.* 500—The List," 140 (see note 11 above).

129 Ibid., 129.

130 Ibid., 132.

131 "Positively Quotable," *Selling Power* (May 2001): 22.

132 Melba Newsome, "The Whole Person Ethic," *Sky* (July 2001): 84.

133 Southwick, "The End of the Fare," 92 (see note 2 above).

134 Amy Larocca, "Gotham," *New York* (August 6, 2001): 10.

135 Robinson, "DollarDEX," 26 (see note 37 above).

136 Tec Fishman, "There Are No Free Wheels," *Esquire* (April 2000): 58–62.

137 Karen Southwick, "The End of the Fare," *Forbes ASAP* (February 21, 2000): 91.

138 Susannah Clark, "People Power," *Continental* (January 2001): 91.

139 Julie Bick, *All I Really Need to Know in Business I Learned at Microsoft* (New York: Pocket Books, 1998).

140 "Job Titles of the Future," *Fast Company* (November 1998): 58.

141 "Job Titles of the Future," *Fast Company* (January 1999): 42.

142 "Job Titles of the Future," *Fast Company* (December 1998): 52.

143 "Dot-coms Learn to Set Sights Lower," *Marin Independent Journal* (July 31, 2001): B1.

144 Silberman, "Just Say Nokia," 135–150, 202 (see note 6 above).

145 Kevin Kelly, "The Roaring Zeros," *Wired* (September 1999): 151–154.

146 Daniel H. Pink, "Land of the Free," *Fast Company* (May 2001): 130.

147 Susan Greco, Christopher Caggiano, and Marc Ballon. "I Was Seduced by the New Economy," *Inc.* (February 1999): 34–57.

148 Marie Rankin Clarke, "Next Stop—the 21st Century," *Fast Company* (September 1999): 112.

Index

About the Author

An award-winning author, speaker, and consultant, Louis Patler is the chairman of Near Bridge, Inc. (www.nearbridge.com), a trends and strategy company that offers "trends-to-profit" consulting, meeting enrichment, services, and training and development programs. Patler brings pioneering technologies for identifying emerging business and consumer trends, practical problem solving, and unparalleled quality-service initiatives to *Fortune 500* companies, multinational corporations, foreign governments, and start-ups alike.

His corporate training programs on *TrendSmart, Innovating for Results*, and new ways of thinking have been delivered to more than thirty thousand executives.

He writes frequent articles for newspapers, magazines, and management newsletters in the U.S. and abroad on the most innovative individuals and companies. England's BBC-TV, SKY-TV, and Canada's CBC-Radio praised him as one of America's new breed of business thought leaders. Recently, the J. Walter Thompson Agency named him one of "The Twenty Most Creative Minds in America." He also hosts a live online chat monthly on www.WorldWithout Borders.com on cutting-edge business topics.

Patler's message is clear and impassioned: the conventional ways of doing business no longer work in the fast-forward, global economy of today. He shows us how to break through old assumptions about leadership, customers, and employees in order to run a *consistently* successful business.

His previous books include *TILT! Irreverent Lessons for Leading Innovation in the New Economy*, which was named a Top 10 Business Book for 1999 by *Management General*. He is also coauthor of the *New York Times* bestseller, *If It Ain't Broke...BREAK IT! and Other*

Unconventional Wisdom for a Changing Business World, which has been widely acclaimed by reviewers such as Tom Peters, Steven Covey, and Paul Hawken; professional coaches Pat Riley and Tony La Russa; and CEOs of *Fortune 500* companies such as Hewlett-Packard and Coca-Cola. It was the second-bestselling business book of 1992. Excerpts from the book have been translated into seventeen languages and have sold twenty-eight million copies. His exciting training programs and videos are based on his three books. *Innovating for Results*, his newest program, is based on *TrendSmart*.

Louis is listed in several national and international *Who's Who* editions, has twice received awards from the National Endowment for the Arts for his writing, and was the editor of the prestigious *American Trend Report*.

A former professional baseball prospect, Louis played on the over-forty World Series Championship team of 2002. He serves on corporate boards and is a member of several community not-for-profit boards. He lives with his wife and children in Marin County, California.

For information on speaking and personal appearances contact:
Kristin Griffin
Literary Services, Inc.
kristin@LiteraryServicesInc.com